ST. LUKE'S MISSIOLOGY

ST. LUKE'S MISSIOLOGY

A Cross-Cultural Challenge

Harold Dollar

William Carey Library

Pasadena, California

Published by
William Carey Library
P.O. Box 40129
Pasadena, California 91114
Telephone (818) 798-0819

Library of Congress Cataloging-in-Publication Data

Dollar, Harold E.
    St. Luke's missiology : a cross-cultural challenge / Harold
Dollar.
        p. cm.
    Includes bibliographical references and index.
    ISBN 0-87808-267-0 (alk. paper)
    1. Bible. N.T. Luke--Criticism, interpretation, etc. 2. Bible.
N.T. Acts--Criticism, interpretation, etc. 3. Missions--History-
-Early church, ca. 30-600. 4. Sociology, Biblical. I. Title.
BS2589.D593   1996
226.4'06--dc20   96-8292
          CIP

---

7 6 5 4 3 2 1
00 99 98 97 96

Printed in the United States of America

Contents

Acknowledgments

There are a number of people that I want to thank for their assistance in enabling me to complete and publish this book. Many of the students at Biola University have read these chapters, listened to my lectures on Acts and critiqued my ideas, both in the classroom and in informal discussions. These students have been undergraduates and graduates, university students and seminary students. Their challenges and suggestions have been of immense help in clarifying my ideas. Michael "Chico" Goff and Bill Hunt have made a number of suggestions that have influenced the structure of the book.

My family has encouraged this project every step along the way. My son Shawn, who is now in the Central African Republic, makes inquiries on my progress in every letter he writes. Sharon, my wife, has read all of this book and given me help each step of the way, including very strong exhortations to finish it and get my ideas out into the market place.

Dr. Michael Wilkins has encouraged me and made specific suggestions on my scholarly development in New Testament studies. Dr. Sherwood Lingenfelter has encouraged me to put my missiological interpretation of Luke-Acts in print. It is due to his encouragement and the specific help of Biola University that this publication will see the light of day.

Finally, I would like to thank my God for Dr. Luke and his phenomenal production of an almost seventy-year story of early Christianity that remains unparalleled in the history of Christianity. This story has captured my mind, and heart and my greatest pleasure is to study and teach this story. My prayer is that those who read this book will better understand the heart of the Triune God, which is a missionary heart.

Introduction

Over the past twenty years of studying and teaching Acts on the mission field and at Biola University, I have become convinced of Luke's importance in understanding early Christianity and the mission of the church today. Commentaries, theological works on Luke-Acts and socio-cultural studies have been immensely helpful in this process. But frequently students miss the missiological contributions Luke makes to the story of early Christianity even when studying good biblical works on Luke-Acts. This study proposes to help readers of Acts in seeing more clearly some of the missiological dimensions of Luke-Acts.

St. Luke's Missiology touches on some of the fundamental contributions of Luke's two-volume work as he tells of how a small Jewish sect became a worldwide movement in one generation. While this book will focus on Acts, section one will recognize the essential unity of Luke-Acts by showing how the Gospel of Luke prepares for the book of Acts. Luke wrote one book in two volumes. There will be a stress on the missiological insights found in Luke's writings. Luke's story of how the gospel moves from the particular to the universal gives insights on the missiological dynamics of early Christianity and provides models for the church and missions today.

1

Who will find the most help from reading this book? Undergraduates and graduates will find this book a helpful supplement in the study of Acts or in giving biblical insights for certain kinds of mission classes, e.g., theology of mission. Missionaries, pastors and lay students will find their understanding of early Christianity and its relevance for today enhanced through this study. Even biblical scholars will be challenged by the missiological dimensions of this book. Although Acts is one of the most missionary books in the Bible, there has been little written on Acts by missiologists. The kinds of issues dealt with in this book will appeal to people who want a serious missiological study of Acts. Throughout this study there will be a focus on the process involved as the gospel moves from the particular to the universal. Another specific purpose of this book is to address some of the issues on frontier missions found in Acts.

While there are numerous publications on Acts ranging from Bible study materials to Greek commentaries, there are almost no books written from a biblical-missiological standpoint. I believe that the particular paradigm I have developed will bring some new insights and sharpen the church's understanding and appreciation of Luke's writings.

St. Luke's Misisology approximates a reader rather than a systematic treatment of Luke-Acts as it explores some of Luke's fundamental themes. Chapter 7 was published in *The International Journal of Frontier Missions* (Dollar 1993c:59-65). All of this study is influenced by *A Biblical-Missiological Exploration of the Crosscultural Dimensions in Luke-Acts* (Dollar 1993b). Although this book is not a systematic treatment of Luke-Acts, there is some continuity of thought as it deals with major themes such as salvation, the mission of the church and the cross-cultural challenge of missions. This book intends to provide a different look at some of these basic themes through the eyes of a missionary who has studied and taught Acts for many years, both on the mission field and in a university context.

The book will explore Luke's missiology in three broad areas. The first division gives an overview of Luke-Acts by looking at how the Gospel of Luke prepares for Acts. This section will demonstrate the essential unity of Luke-Acts. The second section will look at how the gospel, deeply embedded in one particular ethnic group, becomes good news for all peoples. There will be a special focus on the process revealed in Luke's conceptualization of early Christianity. This study will conclude with section three, giving some specific missiological suggestions on how Luke's writings apply to the issue of frontier missions.

PART 1

Overview: Getting the Big Picture

Studying Luke-Acts missiologically as the gospel became universal requires the interpreter to keep in mind the precise nature of Luke's writings. Luke narrates the history of the Christian movement from a religious standpoint. That is, he views the entire story from a divine perspective. Luke uses storytelling to communicate his concerns as a pastor, scholar and participant in early Christianity. Some scholars undervalue Luke's theology because of a misunderstanding of narrative. In concluding his discussion on the contrast between Paul and Luke, Stephen Wilson says:

> We have found that the one thing Luke is not, is a theologian. Insofar as he writes about God, Luke can properly be called a theologian. But this is probably better expressed by saying that Luke's writings are theocentric, rather than by calling him a theologian. For in comparison with the profound, logical and complex theology of Paul, Luke cannot be said to have produced a theology at all. His main interests were historical and practical. . . . [I] conclude that he

was a pastor and a historian rather than a theologian
(1973:255).

Wilson correctly assesses Luke's pastoral concerns while un-
derstating the theological dimension of Luke-Acts. West-
erners assume an epistolary form which flows in a linear,
logical manner for theological reflection. For them Luke's
narrative style cannot be theology. But we should be re-
minded that narrative style is the dominant style within salvation history. Almost all of revelation except the letters in
the New Testament come to us in narrative form. And, even
here, Paul's letters, for instance, flow in a narrative context
and are developed in a story form. The difference in form or
genre does not thereby exclude Luke from being considered
a theologian (Witherington 1994:2). Luke writes the story of
the Christian movement from a religious perspective in a
narrative style. Luke is a theologian, even though his theology does not come to us in a formal or systematic sense
(Fitzmyer 1981:143-270).

Luke will view the entire process of the gospel becoming
universal through a divine lens. For Luke the barriers to the
gospel in the first century were primarily theological. According to him, while universalism is part of the nature of
God and his revelation, God willed that this message be expressed particularistically until the time of Christ. With the
incarnation a wholly new theological ingredient is introduced that will change for all times how and with whom
God will work. While God's message has always been universal, the realization of this universalism (in application)
could not occur until the incarnation.

The theological nature of Luke-Acts diminishes the importance of sociological specifics as this movement moves
from the particular to the universal. But in narrating the story of such a process, Luke does provide a great deal of information that either points to or implies cross-cultural dynamics. In most cases the cross-cultural insights found in
Luke-Acts cannot be deduced by looking for precise sociological statements. Because Luke views everything that hap-

pens from a religious standpoint, his interest in the sociological specifics of the cross-cultural is limited. This understanding is fundamental when interpreting Luke-Acts from a cross-cultural standpoint.

This first section of the book will look at three issues that both link Luke's two volumes and give an overview of his writings. The first chapter will look briefly at the history of the interpretation of Acts and outline five different approaches that have influenced my interpretation of Luke's writings. The second chapter will demonstrate how Luke's overall purpose influenced how he structured volume one and how this purpose would influence the choices he made in the stories he would include. The final chapter of this section will deal with the challenge of change as the gospel moves from a purely Jewish context (particularism) to eventually include the Gentiles (universalism).

1

Interpreting Luke-Acts

Questions to Consider before
Reading this Chapter

*How do *you* interpret Acts? How does your pastor interpret it? How do missionaries use this book? Do we find doctrine in the book of Acts? Or, is Luke only a historical record of the early church?

*If the book of Acts is a missionary story, can we interpret the book adequately without some understanding of missions?

Each book of the Bible requires balanced skills in interpreting its message. Because the Bible is a unique blend of the human and the divine, the interpreter needs objective guidelines, a subjective feel for the writer and his subject, and personal experience in the area being discussed. Luke's writings, which make up some 26% of the New Testament, are especially challenging because his two books cover almost seventy years of the early story of Christianity and moves geographically from Palestine to Rome. While his first volume has many similarities to Matthew and Mark, his second volume contains no parallels. Interpreters have struggled to find a method of interpretation that would do justice to Acts. Luke's second volume is packed with historical, missiological and theological information. How should one go about interpreting Luke's writings and especially his second volume?

I became a Christian in November 1960 while serving in the Air Force in Japan. For the next four years I read through the Bible at least once each year. I always enjoyed reading the book of Acts. My first serious study of Acts occurred during my final year of seminary. My first occasion to teach this book came during my missionary service, first in Trinidad and later in Haiti. Basically I viewed the book of Acts as a history of the early church that provided inspiration and challenge for the church today. It was not primarily a source of doctrine. Doctrine was found in the epistles. Acts, while providing insights on mission and the early history of the church, did not provide theology for the church. As I continued to study and teach Acts it became evident to me that Luke was more than a historian. Finally, about twelve years ago I began to delve deeper into the history of scholarly study of Acts. I wanted to know how the church had interpreted Acts. I found out that most of the critical study of Acts had occurred over the past century and a half.

The History of the Interpretation of Acts

The decisive turning point in the critical study of Luke's second volume can be traced to Ferdinand C. Baur's publications in 1831 and 1845 (Gasque 1975). The past century and a half has seen scholarly study of Acts increase markedly (Mattill 1959; Gasque 1975; Mills 1986; Green and McKeever 1994). The critical study of Acts gradually forced attention back to Luke's first volume and with the publication of Henry Cadbury's study on *The Making of Luke-Acts* (1958) a consensus was reached that Luke wrote only one book, not two.

Producing this one book in two volumes was typical Greco-Roman historiography.

Three clearly distinguished streams of opinion have emerged in the critical study of Acts. The conservative stream, beginning with Matthias Schneckenburger, J. B. Lightfoot and William M. Ramsay all the way down to F. F. Bruce, I. H. Marshall and W. Ward Gasque, focused on the historicity of Acts. Apart from Schneckenburger's early work, those in this stream were reluctant to accept the apologetic nature of Luke-Acts until recent years. This change in the interpre-tation of Acts by evangelicals became pronounced with the publication of Bruce's commentary on Acts (1954; revised 1988). Those of the liberal stream, beginning with Baur and Eduard Zeller and coming down through Martin Dibelius, Hans Conzelmann and Ernst Haenchen, focused on the apologetic or theological nature of Acts.

But there is a third stream falling somewhere in between these two positions. A. von Harnack, F. J. Foakes-Jackson, Kirsopp Lake, Henry J. Cadbury, David B. Barrett, Martin Hengel and recent studies by the Luke-Acts seminar in the Society of Biblical Literature represent this third stream. Most of those in this stream take Luke seriously, especially as a theologian and to a lesser extent as a historian. While at times the debate among these various factions has been rather intense, the overall gain from the various approaches to Acts has produced growing understanding of Luke-Acts and has gradually brought Luke into the limelight of New Testament studies on a par with Paul, John and Peter. Today there is little disagreement over Luke's importance as a theologian in his own right. Indeed, an understanding of the theology of Luke-Acts is vital to a balanced understanding of first-century Christianity.

This book will be an introduction to some of the significant missiological and theological themes in Luke-Acts. Missiology is a relatively new discipline that is in the process of being defined. Some recent attempts to give a precise definition to this discipline have been helpful but not conclusive

(Verkuyl 1978:5; Tippett 1987:XXI-XXV; Scherer 1987:15:4: 507-28). While there is no consensus on a precise definition of missiology, there is some agreement that at least three separate disciplines have made major contributions to the discipline: biblical studies, church history and anthropology. Many other disciplines impact missiology, such as economics, political science, sociology and communications (Tippett 1987:XXV). If missiology could be pictured as a tree, then those disciplines that contribute to its formation would be the roots from which this discipline draws it nurture. A missiological study needs to sensitively integrate theology, church history and anthropology as it goes about its task.

Approaches to the Study of Acts

There are five approaches in biblical studies that have influenced my study of Luke-Acts. All of these approaches, while distinguishable, overlap at a number of points, sometimes stand in tension with one another, but ultimately complement one another.

Five Interpretative Approaches to Acts	
Number	Approach
1	The Historical Veracity of Acts
2	Redactional Studies
3	Luke's Jewishness
4	Narrative Reading
5	Socio-cultural Studies of the NT

The Historical Veracity of Acts

The first of these five approaches are those studies that have attempted to bring their findings within the orbit of the historical veracity of Acts. The most prolific students in this camp in recent decades have been Bruce, Marshall, Gasque and Colin J. Hemer. Another writer that would not hold as firmly to the historicity of all parts of Acts, but who has attempted to defend Luke against the radical criticism that has been a part of German scholarship, is Hengel. He has written two studies in recent years defending the historical credibility of Luke in his story of early Christianity (1980; 1983). Bruce has written two major volumes on Acts (1951, revised in 1990; 1954, revised in 1988). In addition to his two major commentaries on Acts he has written numerous articles on Acts. Marshall has done major work on both Luke and Acts (1970; 1978; 1980). Perhaps the most thorough attempt to defend the historical credibility of Acts is Hemer's recent work (1989).

Evangelicals are increasingly recognizing the theological nature of Luke-Acts, with Marshall giving the title *Luke: Historian and Theologian* to one of his publications (1970). Marshall spends most of this book on the theological themes in Luke-Acts, arguing that salvation is Luke's most prominent theme. Evangelicals are overcoming their apprehension that a focus on the theology of Acts would undermine its historicity.

Redactional Studies

The second area of influence is redactional studies. Redaction describes the contribution of the authors of the books of the New Testament in terms of style, choice of content, structure and even comments by the author. For instance, the book of Acts contains historical information about the early church. But the choice of what went into this book, the conceptualization of how this information would be put together, the style of writing and even the vocabulary used to narrate this story comes out of the mind, heart and spiritual life of the author. Redaction studies attempt to make some type of distinction between the history of the church (tradition) and Luke's contribution to that tradition (redaction). The assumption of this study is that Luke was a real person, living toward the last third of the first century, standing in that Christian community and struggling with the issues facing the church of his day. All of Luke-Acts comes from the pen of Luke and all parts of the book contribute to his overall purpose.

The use of redaction criticism in the study of the Bible is here to stay but there continues to be a great deal of doubt about what is tradition and what is redaction, especially in Acts (Marshall 1970:13-20; Jervell 1972:19-39). This difficulty can be traced back to the findings of Cadbury mentioned above. Cadbury concluded that the style of Luke-Acts was so even and consistent that these two volumes could have but one author. This evenness of style makes it intensely difficult to pinpoint where Luke is creatively constructing and where he is using a source, i.e. traditions of the church. While redaction criticism may be used in Luke's first volume through the use of Matthew and Mark, there are no clearly defined sources in Acts to give this kind of help. But Luke clearly indicates his use of written and oral sources (Lk 1:1-4).

Beverly Roberts Gaventa, for instance, argues that using a redactional approach to defining Luke's theology has been deficient (1988:148). She notes that the lack of known sources, the evenness of Luke's style and the difficulty of determining Luke's purpose, even when discovering tradition, makes this approach inadequate for constructing Lukan theology. Tradition and redaction both ultimately belong to Luke. He is writing the story of the Christian movement out of his own history and the history of the church. What he chooses to include, whether tradition or redaction, contributes to his overall purpose. And since we cannot know for sure where Luke is using sources, it is impossible to make sharp distinctions on the data of Acts.

Luke's Jewishness

A third major influence on this study presents a challenging alternative for interpreting Luke-Acts. These scholars argue that Luke's writings are much more Jewish than previously thought. Jewish influence on the church was dominant throughout the first century (Jervell 1972; 1984; Juel 1983; Esler 1987). These interpreters are saying that Christianity did not become Gentile Christianity during the first century. Jacob Jervell argues, for instance, that the "Jewish" portrait of Paul found in Acts represents, not a Lukan tendency, but rather agrees with the real portrait of Paul which can also be found in the Pauline letters. The church throughout the book of Acts is a Jewish church. According to Jervell no Gentile church nor Gentile mission can be found in Luke's narrative. While Jervell may at times overstate the Jewishness of Luke's writings, his attempt to rewrite the history of early Christianity is not as absurd as it may sound. Jervell and those like him have rightly challenged Luke's interpreters to recognize the significant role played by Jewish Christians during the entire first century of the Christian movement.

Narrative Reading

A fourth approach comes from those using narratology as a way of arriving at a balanced interpretation of Luke-Acts (Talbert 1974; Johnson 1977;Tannehill 1986; 90; Gaventa 1986). Narrative reading is defined and illustrated by Gaventa (1986:146-57). This approach requires that the interpreter keep in mind the entire two volumes when interpreting any particular theme or idea in Luke-Acts. Gaventa begins her article by outlining some of the weaknesses of past approaches to finding the theology of Luke. She points out the specific inadequacies of each of these methodologies, arguing that "what is missing from all of these methods is some attempt to deal seriously with the character of Acts as a narrative" (1986:149). These methodologies are built upon presuppositions that lead one to focus on only particular parts of Luke's writings. Gaventa argues that Luke wrote a complete story and that all parts of his story, whether speeches, themes, history, or redaction, are important, but only in the context of the whole story. It is only in rereading that one can discover Luke's theology.

The advantage of viewing Luke-Acts as a narrative unity is that this methodology is characterized by holistic thinking. Luke's two volumes cover over twenty-five percent of the New Testament and almost seventy years of history. The story moves from the heart of Judaism at the beginning of the century and ends in Rome within a Gentile context in AD 62. It touches on so many themes and contains so much information that it is easy when studying some particular theme or part of Luke-Acts to neglect the larger context. It is most difficult to keep in mind all of the data of Luke-Acts when developing any one particular idea. Narrative reading challenges the interpreter to be mindful of the whole. As Gaventa says: "An attempt to do justice to the theology of Acts must struggle to reclaim the character of Acts as a narrative" (1986:150).

Socio-cultural Studies

The fifth influence on this study is sociological explorations of early Christianity. These studies demonstrate the importance of taking seriously the socio-cultural dynamics of the first century Jewish and Greco-Roman worlds when interpreting the New Testament. While there was some interest in the sociological approach to the New Testament at the beginning of this century, the past few decades have seen a renewed interest in this approach (Kee 1989:1-6). The application of this discipline offers an opportunity for shedding new light on the origin and development of early Christianity. It has already produced a number of sociological studies of the New Testament (Judge 1960; Berger and Luckmann 1966; Smith 1975:19-21; Gager 1975; Theissen 1978; Scroggs 1980:164-79; Tidball 1984; Esler 1987; Kee 1989).

These studies range from an attempt to provide a social history of early Christianity all the way to studies which give a generic ethnography of the first-century Greco-Roman world (Judge 1960; Malina 1981). Peter Berger and Thomas Luckmann's contribution to an understanding of social structure and Berger's application of these insights to religion are among the most helpful models for understanding the New Testament world (1966; 1967). For instance, they argue that one of the functions of a new movement is that of legitimation (Berger and Luckmann 1967:92-128). This usually occurs in the second generation of the movement. Following this reasoning, Luke-Acts legitimizes Christianity by showing its vital connection to the Old Testament and its acceptance by Roman rulers.

Gerd Theissen's study, using a conflict model which focuses on the political, social and economic pressures on the Jews in Palestine, provides insight into the dynamics of the Jesus movement in its beginnings (1978). Apart from Malina's work, the application of the discipline of anthropology in New Testament studies has been limited primarily to some use of symbolic anthropology and especially to insights stemming from the publications of Mary Douglas (Malina 1986; Lingenfelter 1992). Her theory, that a culture's rules on eating and sex are influenced by its cosmology, proves helpful in understanding the manner in which Jewish food laws and their prohibitions on who could enter the Temple functioned as boundary-marking activities.

Methodological Considerations

This study will examine some key missiological and theological themes from Luke's two volumes. Luke traces the story from the center of particularism (Judaism) until it becomes solidly established in the universal (Jew and Gentile). There are a few terms used in a number of chapters in this book that need to be defined. These definitions will also enable the reader to understand some of the methodology used in this study. The first two of these terms, Judaism and particularism, are interrelated. Neither Luke nor any other New Testament writer ever uses the term Judaism. Although the NRSV and the NIV translate the word Ἰουδαϊσμῶ in Galatians 1:13 and 14 as Judaism, the stress here is on Paul's Jewishness, not on Judaism as the name for a religious system (Gütbrod 1985:375). In fact there is an ongoing debate

today as whether it is appropriate to use Judaism for anything other than that expression of the Jewish faith that came
into existence after the fall of Jerusalem in AD 70.

This study recognizes that there was tremendous diversity within the Jewish world of the first century just as
there is today. There were many different parties among the
Jews of the first century with widely differing religious and
theological views (Hengel 1974; Theissen 1984; Porton
1986:57-80; Josephus 1987). Some of the best known are the
Pharisees, Essenes, Sadducees and the political revolutionaries, but there were many other lesser-known groups
inside and outside Palestine (Porton 1986:57-80).

The word *particularism* focuses on the cultural dimensions of Judaism while recognizing that in a historical sense
the grace of God was provided through the elect Jewish people. Although there were numerous parties and beliefs within the Judaism of the first century there was a firm belief
among all committed Jews that there was a sharp distinction,
religiously and culturally, between themselves and Gentiles.
This distinction was associated in the Jewish mind with their
dietary laws, with circumcision and especially in the particularity of the Temple where this distinction was spelled
out visually, verbally and practically. With all of the di-
vergent views on what a Gentile had to do to become an orthodox Jew, ultimately a Gentile were required to make significant cultural changes in order to become a proselyte to
Judaism (*The Antiquity of the Jews*, 1987:526-28; Segal
1988:336-69). The word "particular" points to the belief that
if Gentiles embraced the Jewish faith they also had to embrace Jewish biblical forms, i.e. Jewish culture, that required
them to leave their Gentile culture. Christianity began as a
movement among Palestinian and diaspora Jews and gradually moved into the Gentile world as a faith for all peoples
irrespective of cultural distinctions.

A third word of importance in this study is the word
universalism. This word is used in two quite different but
overlapping ways in this study. Universalism is a fundamental word in a biblical theology of mission and refers to

God's redemptive concern and commitment to all peoples. So, for instance, when referring to the universalism found in Luke's first volume this is the primary way this word will be used. The second usage, and the dominant one in this study, places the emphasis on the cultural dimensions. It indicates that the Christian faith has moved beyond one cultural expression, i.e., the particular. The writer of Ephesians refers to this process in terms of a huge dividing wall being taken down between Jews and Gentiles (Eph 2:12-21). Luke speaks of Jews and Gentiles having table-fellowship together. Universalism in this study will concentrate on the cultural barriers being removed as people respond to the good news. In this sense, it indicates that the gospel is no longer bound up with any one cultural and/or ethnic group. The gospel that has always been universal in divine intent now becomes universal in application. Practically, this means that Jews can become Christians while retaining their Jewish identity and Gentiles can become Christians while retaining their Gentile identity.

Personal Response and Reflection

1. Which of these five approaches to the study of Acts would be most helpful to you right now? Why?

2. How will the terms particularism and universalism be used in this book? How do these terms apply to you and your church?

3. State in your own words what this book intends to accomplish. What is its fundamental purpose(s)?

2

From Particularism to Universalism

Questions to Consider before Reading this Chapter

*How many different ethnic groups live in your immediate neighborhood? How many of your friends come from ethnic groups different from your own?

*You have been asked to join an outreach ministry to those in your community who have been overlooked by your church in the past. How would you go about preparing to fulfill this mission?

The post-WWII Cold War between East and West has ended. Nuclear holocaust is no longer an ominous threat to humankind. But a different kind of threat to the world has come to the front. This threat can be traced back to Babel. Throughout the world today violence between groups is escalating. Almost every day our newspapers and television newscasts headline these atrocities. Literally thousands are dying each week. What is so deceptive about the size of the problem is that the number of deaths are rather small in most cases. Fifty in South Africa, twenty-five in Nigeria, fifteen in Israel, sixty in Yugoslavia and a hundred in the U.S. These small numbers add up to huge numbers when put together. Along with these many examples of small numbers being killed, there is the occasional Rwanda where a million or more are killed in a very short period of time. This new manifestation of violence stems from ethnic, religious, social, economic and ideological differences.

These kinds of conflict were also evident in the first-century Greco-Roman world. Rome's military might and brilliant administrative skills brought some unity to the world of that day, yet they could not solve the tensions between people. In fact they perpetuated it. "The social pyramid of ancient Rome was a great deal higher and steeper than those of the most highly developed European countries today . . ." (Grant 1960:87). Socially the empire was divided into citizens, freedmen and slaves; culturally there were Romans, Greeks and barbarians with many other sub-groups. There were those within the Roman Empire who maintained their cultural identity in the midst of these vast peoples. Among the most distinctive of these groups were the Jews. Even the Roman government granted them some level of cultural and religious autonomy (Sanders 1992).

Out of this context a messianic movement arose that would cross all of the religious, cultural, economic, social and gender boundaries during the first century. Luke makes it clear that God willed that his revelation should be made known to the world through a religiously and culturally particular group. That particular group came to be known as the Jewish people and their religion as Judaism. When Luke begins his narrative of this movement, the Jewish people, while scattered throughout the Roman Empire, have their religious center in ancient Palestine. In spite of being dominated by Gentiles for more than five centuries this people had maintained, with various degrees of success, its historic particularism. Although the Judaism of the first century is quite pluralistic, with a diversity of theological and organizational expressions, most Jews maintained some sharp distinction between themselves and non-Jews.

Luke demonstrates that the Jesus movement, originating out of this Jewish particularism, became a universal movement within one generation. Jews, Gentiles and Samaritans could become a part of God's people without losing their cultural identity. He also asserts that this was God's will. Many Jews and Christians had doubts about these changes and resisted them all along the way. But gradually and imperceptibly God worked out his will and within three decades a movement that had been deeply imbedded in particularism had become radically universal.

How did this occur? How did this movement begun by a young Galilean Jew become a worldwide movement in such a short period of time? It might be assumed that the answer to this question cannot be found in Luke's first volume. When the Gospel of Luke ends the movement started under Jesus' leadership remained Jewish and was limited to Palestine. But, in spite of appearances, the seeds of universalism had been liberally watered by Jesus and would sprout and grow into a huge tree in a few short decades after his death.

Luke's two-volume narrative traces the early Christian movement as it moves from a single-culture/people to a multi-culture/peoples. This represents one of the most revolutionary and difficult changes in the entire story of salvation history. It was a time of identity crisis for this new movement as its adherents struggled to discover who they were in relationship to Judaism and the larger Greco-Roman culture. Today's global search for guidelines on dealing with the ethnic, religious and social divisions that have come to prominence in the post-Cold War world could profit from a study of early Christianity. The changes this early church went through provide insights for Christians throughout the world.

This chapter will give an overview of how Luke's first volume lays a foundation for the universalization of Christianity. After the prologue to his book (Lk 1:1-4), Luke plunges his reader into the heart of the Jewish religious system of the first century (Lk 1:5ff.). John the Baptist is the son of a priest who serves in the Temple in Jerusalem. Jesus is the son of a very devout Jewish woman and his family raises him as an orthodox Jew. In fact, as Luke demonstrates, Jesus remained strictly within the Jewish faith and his ministry was limited to those living within Palestine. He carried out his ministry within the religious guidelines of the Scripture. While it can be said that Luke's first volume is characterized by universalism, it is a universalism that is sharply distinguished from Mark and Matthew at key points. For instance, while Luke seems to follow much of Mark's gospel, he omits Mark 13:10 and 14:9 where Mark says explicitly that the gospel will be proclaimed through the world. Luke also omits Mark 7:1-29 where Mark shows that the the Jewish food laws are obsolete and where Jesus heals the child of a Gentile woman. Is there any explanation for these omissions and the general reluctance of Luke to bring the issue of worldwide mission explicitly to the foreground in his first volume? Yes. Luke's purpose to write one book in two volumes influenced the choices he made for the content of each volume.

Paradigm: A Model for Studying the Gospel of Luke

Luke deliberately chooses those parts of the life of Christ that will provide a foundation for the mission to the Gentiles. In order to demonstrate how and why Luke prepares for this eventuality, I will use Thomas Kuhn's concept of paradigm to analyze the Gospel of Luke (1970). Kuhn says that scientific knowledge develops, grows and is governed by paradigms. A paradigm implicitly defines what the legitimate problems are along with the orthodox methods of carrying out research in a given field. It provides the parameters and tells how problems will be researched and solved. He illustrates this by citing a number of paradigms that have been influential in the past, such as the Copernican revolution and the Newtonian theory. The paradigm that removed Earth from the center of the cosmos and theorized that it rotated around the sun answered baffling questions that had plagued scientists for generations and at the same time opened up multiple problem-solving possibilities in understanding the universe. This paradigm and others mentioned by Kuhn were successful in explaining natural phenomena that previously had baffled the scientific community. At the same time they offered new horizons to the scientific community for problem-solving. How do new paradigms come into existence and replace old ones?

How New Paradigms Begin

New paradigms come into existence because of mental agitation created by the failure of the dominant paradigm to explain the major issues and resolve the central problems in any particular scientific field. Kuhn refers to the unsolved problems that produce this agitation as anomalies (1970:52). Scientific communities give up the "normal" paradigm when the following two criteria are met. First, there must be a large number of unsolved problems in the dominant paradigm coupled with a high degree of intensity so as to cause mental anxiety at one's inability to resolve these problems. Second, there must be a new paradigm available that gives promise of resolving these tensions and, at the same time, opens up new problem-solving opportunities. If the first condition is met but no new paradigm is available, then the scientific community will usually ignore the anomalies, rationalize them away or confess to the inadequacies of their present knowledge while holding to the normal paradigm.

To illustrate how anomalies create this tension Kuhn draws upon an experiment performed by Bruner and Postman in the field of psychology (1970:62). In this experiment subjects were asked to identify playing cards through short periods of exposure. Unknown to the subject a certain percentage of the cards had been changed so as to measure mental perception and reaction. For instance, a five of spades (black) might be colored red. Some of the subjects would identify it as a spade, while others would call it a heart. Through increased exposure most of the subjects would eventually identify all of the cards correctly. But, in the process, almost all subjects experienced some measure of mental agitation while undergoing the experiment. One of them even went so far as to exclaim: "I can't make the suit out, whatever it is. It didn't even look like a card that time. I don't know what color it is now or whether it's a spade or a heart. I'm not even sure now what a spade looks like. My God!" (1970:63-64).

Application of Paradigm to Luke's Writings

These insights from Kuhn can be applied profitably to the social sciences, the humanities and biblical studies. For instance, the reaction of the apostles when Jesus told them he was going to Jerusalem to die is understandable when seen as a paradigm conflict (Lk 9:22, 43-45; 18:31-34 with 19:11; 24:21). In spite of his repeated attempts to convince his disciples that he was going to Jerusalem and would be killed, they could not understand what he was saying. How can their incomprehension be explained? The disciples of Jesus were convinced that Jesus was God's promised Messiah. According to their understanding (paradigm), the Messiah would be a triumphant ruler who would overthrow all opposition to God. He would establish God's rule on earth. This was a fundamental paradigm in their understanding of Scripture. Thus Jesus' statement that he was going to die was anomalous. It did not fit their theological messianic paradigm.

While there was a great deal of diversity within first-century Jewish faith (Pharisees, Essenes, Zealots, Sadducees), the dominant paradigm of this faith required some sharp distinction between Jews and Gentiles. But at the same time Israel's faith was rooted in a universalism that called for all nations of the earth to acknowledge the uniqueness of Yahweh. Jesus was socialized into this paradigm. He was circumcised on the eighth day, attended the synagogue and Temple, and was, in general, an orthodox Jew. How could Jesus maintain his commitment to this particularism and at the same time prepare his disciples for the time when they would preach to Gentiles and eventually even fellowship with them? He prepared his disciples by challenging the particularism of his day.

There were many things in the life and ministry of Jesus that were anomalous and that challenged the boundaries of the dominant paradigm of the day. All of the gospels demonstrate, for instance, how Jesus went beyond what was considered appropriate behavior for a devout person in Jewish society in the first century. Jesus constantly demonstrated an affinity for those whom the Pharisees regarded as marginal in the social and religious life of Israel. While this theme is found in all of the gospels, there are indications that this dimension of Jesus' ministry provided Luke with an oblique and discreet way of preparing his reader for the eventual inclusion of the Gentiles. As a result Luke gives a great deal more attention to this aspect of Jesus' ministry than do the authors of the other synoptics. Using the concept of anomaly, I will point out four categories of anomalies found in Luke's narrative of Jesus' ministry. These anomalies caused a great deal of mental agitation among almost all Jews. But for Luke's purpose a focus on these aspects of Jesus' ministry and life lay the foundation for the universalization of the Christian movement.

The Anomalies of Luke

The anomalies Luke presents are in the form of stories Jesus told and relationships he had during his ministry. Many of the people Jesus associated with were on the periphery of Jewish society. Luke shows an inordinate interest in women, sinners and tax collectors, the poor, the helpless, Samaritans and others who came seeking his help. Much of the material unique to Luke includes stories about these kinds of people. The four categories of anomalies I will trace are sinners and tax collectors, women, Samaritans and the so-called quest stories.

Sinners and Tax Collectors

"Behold, a glutton and a drunkard, a friend of tax collectors and sinners!" (7:34) could have been an epitaph on Jesus' grave according to Luke's gospel. Those who were regarded as marginal in Jewish society were attracted to Jesus. Luke first introduces the possibility of this kind of frontier ministry in Jesus' programmatic statement in 4:16-30. Later, when Levi becomes one of the Twelve, the social and religious implications of this radical change comes forcefully to the front (5:27ff.). When Jesus calls him to be one of his disciples, Levi throws a going-away party where he invites "a large company of tax collectors" along with Jesus and his disciples (5:29). This immediately raises questions in the minds of the local religious leaders as to what motive Jesus could have for attending such a questionable gathering. This in turn prompted Jesus to state: "I have not come to call the righteous, but sinners to repentance" (v. 32). This accent on sinners finding repentance became a dominant theme in Luke's gospel from that point onward.

Recent studies agree that Jesus had an unusual relationship with those who were regarded as on the margins of Jewish life. E. P. Sanders, for instance, says: "The promise of salvation to sinners is the undeniably distinctive characteristic of Jesus' message" (1985:174). Marshall agrees with this when he says: "Within Israel itself it is a matter of plain historical fact, admitted by all, that Jesus ate with the tax-collectors and sinners, and thus demonstrated the love of God to them" (1970:138).

The oppressiveness of the Roman tax system, coupled with Jews collecting these taxes, proved to be a source of constant irritation within Palestine. Jewish tax collectors were terribly offensive to all Jews and especially to the Pharisees. Theissen's observation, that the Jesus movement was characterized by a radical love that distinguished it from all other movements in early first-century Palestine, is nowhere more sharply exemplified than in Jesus' relationship to sinners and tax collectors (1985:97-110). Thus Luke's statement that "the tax collectors and sinners were all drawing near to hear him" and that the Pharisees and the scribes consequently murmured, makes sense when looked at in the sociological context of first-century Palestine. Numerous examples of how this model has influenced Christianity could also be drawn from the history of the church. For example, the early success of Pentecostals in reaching the poor, notorious social outcasts and the marginals in early twentieth-century America and the reaction of the mainline churches to this movement illustrates that the response of the Pharisees was not, in fact, so atypical, even when compared with a relatively neutral sociological context (Harrell, Jr. 1975:2, 18-19, 42). This ministry of Jesus to tax collectors represents an anomaly in the dominant paradigm of particularism.

Women

As the consciousness of people in the Western world has risen regarding the equality of women, so Luke's portrait of Jesus' relationship to women becomes even more striking. But the modern reader of Luke may not be aware of how radical Jesus' conduct was and may assume that the prominence of women in his first volume represents the normal view of women in first century Palestine. Joachim Jeremias says (1969:359):

> Eastern women take no part in *public life*. This was true of Judaism in the time of Jesus, in all cases where Jewish families faithfully observed the Law. When the Jewess of Jerusalem left her house, her face was hidden by an arrangement of two head veils, a head-band on the forehead with bands to the chin, and a hairnet with ribbons and knots, so that her features could not be recognized. It was said that once, for example, a chief priest in Jerusalem did not recognize his own mother when he had to carry out against her the prescribed process for a woman suspected of adultery.

This picture is somewhat overstated and represents something of a caricature as Jeremias himself admits later, especially in the rural areas where women worked in the fields and carried water from wells. But there is little doubt that women were relegated to the margins of public life, whether religious, political, social or educational. Bruce J. Malina, using an anthropological model of honor and shame, shows that in first-century Greco-Roman culture females functioned and had meaning only in relationship to males (1981:42-47). Women were not expected to, and often were positively discouraged from, getting any kind of formal education (Jeremias 1969:363). Further, women were not to speak to men in public and they were not expected to move very far from their homes unless under the sponsorship of a male.

In light of this information it is quite striking to discover the amount of information on women in the Gospel of Luke and the prominence he gives to them in the Jesus movement. Luke begins his narrative by focusing on the vital role played by Elizabeth and Mary in the beginning of the gospel story (Lk 1–2; compare Mt 1–2). He then ends his account in chapter 24 with women being the first disciples to know of the resurrection (24:1ff.). Women play a prophetic role in the birth of John and Jesus, in the dedication of Jesus, in supporting his ministry (8:1-3) and at his crucifixion (23:55,56).

One of the most startling instances of Jesus' radical departure from the norm of the day is revealed in the story of Mary and Martha (10:38-42). Here Jesus turns the traditional understanding of women completely on its head. Marshall says that "Mary's posture [sitting] expresses zeal to learn (cf. K. Weiss, TDNT VI, 630), and it is significant that Jesus encourages a woman to learn from him since the Jewish teachers were generally opposed to this . . . " (1978:452). Mary is held up as a model of womanly virtue by her interest in being a student-disciple, one who studies God's word. At the same time, by reminding us that Jesus contrasted her favorably to Martha, Luke relativizes the whole domestic role. A similar pattern can be seen in 11:27-28 when in reply to a woman's exuberant exclamation that the woman who bore him was blessed, Jesus replied: "Blessed rather are those who hear the word of God and keep it." Jesus, in this way, makes the role of motherhood submissive to discipleship.

But perhaps the most striking of all of Luke's references to women is found in 8:1-3 where, in giving a generalized summary of Jesus' activity, Luke tells of some women who were traveling with Jesus. Verse one indicates that Jesus is engaged in a campaign of preaching all through Galilee and he has the Twelve (men) assisting him. Then verses two and three name some women who also accompanied him. He names three in particular—Mary, Joanna, Susanna—and then says that there were "many others." Luke says that these women "provided for them out of their means." E. Earle Ellis says: "Like the Apostles, they also are witnesses in Galilee as well as at the crucifixion and resurrection" (1966:24). Women, who were regarded as marginal in Jewish life, are brought to the center of life in the new movement founded by Jesus of Nazareth.

Samaritans

Luke first introduces the Samaritans as Jesus leaves Galilee and sets out for Jerusalem (9:51-56). This is the first of four appearances of the Samaritans in Luke's story; two of the other three are also found in the gospel (10:25-37; 17:11-19); and the fourth one is found in Acts (8:4-24). Luke shows a greater interest in the Samaritans than any other biblical writer.

Jeremias' study on "The Maintenance of Racial Purity" shows that within Jewish society the Samaritans were at the bottom of the scale in racial purity, even below Gentiles (1969:252-58; 271-76). He traces the ups and downs of this relationship from the Assyrian captivity in the eighth century B.C. to the second century A.D. While there were periods when the tensions between Jews and Samaritans were not so severe, the first century was not one of those periods. He says: "Thus, in the first century AD with which we are now

concerned, we are in one of the periods of embittered relationships between Jews and Samaritans" (1969:354).

In light of the general avoidance of the Samaritans by
the other synoptics, why does Luke show such an interest in
them? Luke first introduces the Samaritans in Luke 9:51-56
in the context of Jesus' intention to go to Jerusalem. He
leaves Galilee and heads for Jerusalem, sending his disciples
ahead into Samaria to prepare for his coming. Luke says that
"the people would not receive him, because his face was set
toward Jerusalem" (v. 53).

When two of Jesus' disciples suggest that the appropriate response to this Samaritan rejection should be modeled
after Elijah's ministry—"Lord, do you want us to bid fire
come down from heaven and consume them?"—along with
Jesus' response—"But he turned and rebuked them"—the
reader arrives at a more complete understanding of the passage. While this does not take the sting out of the Samaritans' rejection of Jesus it does indicate the point Luke is
making. Jesus is correcting the attitude of hostility and ven-
geance characteristic of Jews toward Samaritans.

The second reference to the Samaritans, similarly, and
even more devastatingly, reveals the deficiencies in the rel-
igiosity of the Jews when compared to the Samaritans (10:26-
37). Literarily this masterpiece of Lukan artistry provides
one of the most memorable and powerful stories to be found
in all of biblical literature. Jesus confronts the tendency of
faith to lose touch with human need. Two of the most orthodox and religious groups within Israel, whose primary
function should be the meeting of human needs, are compared to an ordinary Samaritan and in a context in which a
Samaritan might be least responsive to human needs, i.e.,
within Israel proper and close to Jerusalem. Unlike the Jewish priest and Levite who show themselves uncaring and
compassionless, the Samaritan is instantly moved by compassion and stops all of his activity to assist his fellow man.

Luke's third reference to Samaritans comes in a su-
prising context (17:11-19). Ten lepers seek Jesus out for healing. Jesus heals them and sends them to a Jewish priest. One

of the ten turns back and begins to worship and praise his benefactor, bowing at Jesus' feet. This thankful one of the ten is a Samaritan (v.16). Jesus then registers a combination of shock and surprise when he says: "Was no one found to return and give praise to God except this foreigner . . . your faith has saved you" (vv. 18-19).

The Quest Stories

Robert C. Tannehill's literary studies of Luke-Acts brings to the surface another element of Luke's creativity in bringing before his readers the extent to which Jesus was concerned for the marginals in his day. He says that the synoptic writers constantly use pronouncement stories as a way of conveying who Jesus was and what he taught. "Synoptic pronounce-ment stories are brief narratives which report how Jesus responded in words (and sometimes also in action) to something said or observed on a particular occasion" (1986:111). These pronouncement stories can be classified under the rubrics of correction, commendation, objection, inquiry and quest stories (111-27). The fifth type, the quest story, is the one Tannehill particularly develops. Tannehill focuses on the quest stories found in the gospel of Luke. These are stories where someone approaches Jesus in search of something that is extremely important to his or her well-being. There are normally obstacle(s) in the way which build suspense and the reader awaits the outcome of the person's encounter with Jesus. These stories are usually resolved with Jesus graciously meeting their needs.

Of the seven quest stories found in Luke four are unique to him and six of the seven concern individuals who seemed most unlikely to qualify for Jesus' help. All six of these apparently "unqualified" individuals find answers to their need (1986:113). The seventh, and the only "failure," concerns a rich young ruler, who, in the eyes of Jesus' disciples, was already a success (18:18-30).

The Quest Stories		
Number	Text	Story
1	Luke 5:17-26	A Sinful Paralytic
2	Luke 7:1-10	A Gentile Centurion
3	Luke 7:36-50	A Sinful Woman
4	Luke 17:11-19	A Samaritan Leper
5	Luke 19:1-10	A Chief Tax Collector
6	Luke 23:39-43	A Crucified Criminal
7	Luke 18:18-30	A Rich Young Ruler

Some of these quest stories are also included in the three anomalies already discussed. The sinful woman, the Samaritan leper and the chief tax collector are also found in the previous anomalies. These three stories, along with the crucified criminal, are all unique to Luke's gospel. The striking aspect of these stories when looked at together is the theme of reversal. In six of these stories the people would be considered marginal, i.e., outside the dominant paradigm of particularism. Only one, the rich young ruler, would be considered well within the dominant paradigm of first century Jewish particularism. In the case of the six "marginals" Jesus responds with compassion and without delay grants them their request, thereby including them in his definition of particularism. The one person that the reader expected should be granted his request is denied. The disciples are utterly baffled that Jesus sends this rich man away sorrowful (Lk 18:26). This reaction gives some indication of the mental agitation they were experiencing.

34   ST. LUKE'S MISSIOLOGY

Conclusion

God chose to make his will known through a particular people (Gn 12:1-3). His revelation to the world came through the Jews. The Mosaic law defined Israel both religiously and culturally. There was no distinction between their faith and their culture. God gave them circumcision, the cultic rituals and guidelines on what to eat. Jews were required to distinguish between themselves and other peoples. They were constantly challenged to "come out from among them and be separate."

As the Jews embraced this revelation and began their pilgrimage they experienced a great deal of tension. This tension manifested itself in the inherent universalism of their calling. The God who made them a people also willed that through the Jews all the peoples of the earth would be blessed. How could they be true to these two callings: One to be particular and the other to embrace their universalism? Throughout Jewish history these two callings became increasingly complex and difficult to hold in tension. The book of Jonah speaks directly to this issue. The message of Jonah is that the Jews had abandoned their universal mission. During the intertestamental period the influence of Greek culture almost led them to deny their Jewishness (Hengel 1973). For many Jews the only option was to focus on their calling to be separate. The development of parties such as Pharisees, Essenes and Sadducees helped Israel define what a good Jew should look like.

The Judaism into which Jesus was born was not just the particularism of the Scriptures but a particularism that had developed out of Jewish history. So, in a sense, Jesus did not challenge Jewish biblical particularism, rather he challenged first-century Jewish particularism. Note carefully in this regard that the people Jesus ministered to were Jews in most cases. The sinners and tax collectors were Jews. Even the Samaritans were monotheistic Palestinians. But in terms of the dominant paradigm of the first century these people were outside the pale. What Jesus did was to go back to the particularism of the Scriptures. The origin of the Jewish people was God's selection of a people who were marginal. They were powerless and unable to help themselves. They were a slave people. Jesus simply returns to that model of compassion and justice found in the exodus event. Luke's selection of those groups Jesus ministered to are anomalous in the normal paradigm of first-century Jewish particularism.

The universalism found in Luke does not place the Gentiles at the very center of Jesus' mission theology. But the prominence marginals have in the life and ministry of Jesus laid a foundation for the eventual inclusion of Gentiles. In this way, Luke, while neglecting some of the more obvious statements about the Gentiles found in Matthew and Mark, prepares for the time when the messianic movement will be universalized.

The nature of Jesus' ministry in the first century should be a challenge for the church and the world today. Churches tend to define themselves particularistically, thereby erecting barriers between people based on social, religious, ethnic and gender differences. Jesus reached out and touched people both within and outside the normal paradigm of his day. His actions were seen as anomalous in his day. Can the church exemplify this anomalous behavior today?

Personal Response and Reflection

1. Define the words *paradigm* and *anomaly* and show how they are used in this chapter.

2. Does Luke show Jesus engaging in mission particularistically or universalistically?

3. In what ways were Jesus' relationships to tax collectors, women and Samaritans anomalous?

4. Name and discuss briefly a relationship within your community that might be anomalous to the members of your church.

3
The Challenge of Change

Questions to Consider before
Reading this Chapter

*Your church uses exclusively contemporary music, accompanied by such instruments as guitars, synthesizers and drums in the worship service. Some of your new members are requesting traditional hymns with the piano. As a music leader of this church, how would you bring about change to accommodate these new members?

*What do you think is the best example of change that you have seen made in your church during the past two years?

The American myth of John Henry, a black railroad worker, who battles a steel-driving machine with brute force provides a fascinating study of change. The setting of the story takes place during the construction of the Big Bend tunnel on the Chesapeake & Ohioan in West Virginia during the 1870s. As the story goes, the railroad company brought a new machine out to the work site. It was a new experimental drill, driven by steam. When tunnelling through the mountains, holes had to be drilled into the rock so that dynamite could be inserted to blow off large chunks of rock. Human force was normally used for this drilling. A worker had to swing a ten-pound hammer all day.

The work crew immediately felt threatened when the foreman told them what the ugly contraption was supposed to do. The men started talking and John Henry offered to challenge this machine to a contest. John Henry took a *twenty*-pound hammer in each hand and for the next thirty-five minutes he and the machine drove steel. At the end of this time John Henry had driven two seven-foot holes and the machine had driven one nine-foot hole.

Children read this American myth and often go away with the victory of John Henry fixed firmly in their mind. But they don't really hear the end of the story. John Henry overexerts himself and dies soon after his "victory." The real lesson of the story is the inevitability of technological change. To resist this change is not simply to be mistaken, it can result in death. It also illustrates a universal: the most natural response to change is resistance. This, of course, is not all bad because some change is harmful and should be resisted. But change itself is inevitable.

Change is a biological, sociological, psychological, economic and political fact of life. All of creation is constantly going through change. Some change is constructive and some change is destructive. For example, at one time Haiti was one of the most productive countries in the colonial world. Today it is the poorest country in the Western hemisphere. At one time the waters of the Atlantic would sweep in and inundate large areas of Holland and wreak havoc on land and people. Today, destructive flooding is almost unknown in Holland. All change is somewhat threatening, both to nature and to people. Psychologists have developed a scale to measure stress that looks at stress as a product of change. They give points to such things as job change, mar-

riage, death in the family, moving to a new location, gradua-
tion and job promotion. The more serious the change, e.g.,
the death of a spouse, the greater the stress. But what is interesting in this scale is that even good change, e.g., marriage, increases stress. Both change and stress are inevitable.

A Period of Intense Change

The period of time between the birth of Jesus and the
separation of the Christian church from the Jewish synagogue represents a period of incredible change. This radical
change affected the total life of those involved, especially
Jews and those who normally attended the synagogue. Luke
shows a great deal of interest in this change. His two-volume
narrative of early Christian history provides one of the most
fascinating case studies of this change. The challenge of
change revealed in Luke's story is the subject of this chapter.
We will began with an exposition of the fundamental principles of change as given by Jesus himself in Luke 5:33-39.
Following this exposition will be a case study of how this
works out in Acts.

Overview of Luke 5:33-39

This story, found very early in Jesus' ministry in all
three gospels, lays a foundation for understanding Jesus' relationship to Judaism and for understanding the relationship
between messianic Christianity and Judaism throughout his
second volume.

Three Religious Groups

This story brings three different religious groups face to
face over a religious practice. All of them are Jewish and are
committed to the Jewish law. Each of these groups would be
considered agents of change. They would be only three
groups out of the many within first-century Judaism. Each of
these groups addressed the basic questions that Israel was

facing during this time: how should the Law be interpreted and applied in a situation where a pagan empire is controlling Palestine? What posture should a Jew have toward the Roman government? Submission? Passive resistance? Violent resistance?

The Disciples of the Pharisees

The oldest and best known of the three groups introduced here is the Pharisees. While precise knowledge of the Pharisees is somewhat scarce, there are three basic sources of knowledge of early first century Pharisaism (Neusner 1984). The earliest source would be the gospels written some thirty to sixty years after the events they record. These gospels are not written to give historical information about the Pharisees but are written by partisans of Christianity. The second source of knowledge would be Josephus, a Jewish historian captured and taken to Rome at the fall of Jerusalem in AD 70. He wrote a history of the Jews during the last decade of the first century. The third source would be the Jewish writings, known as the Midrash, written during the third century. These writings are by the Pharisees who claim that their laws go back to Gamaliel in the first century. But there is no way of knowing if, in fact, these laws represent accurately the belief of early first-century Pharisaism (Sanders 1992:ix-xi).

What we do know from the gospels is that the Pharisees had a specific understanding of the Law and how it should be applied to daily life. They placed a great deal of emphasis on observable conduct, believing that the religious state of a person could be determined by his/her external actions. They were very influential throughout Palestine through their presence in the synagogues. Josephus estimates that there were only about 6,000 members (*Antiquities* 18.2.4). They had very stringent rules for membership and considered themselves the guardians of religious orthodoxy. Change should come in terms of the religious laws they developed. These laws, if followed, would maintain ritual purity and prevent contamination by Gentiles and sinners and prepare for the Messiah.

The Disciples of John the Baptist

The second group is the disciples of John the Baptist. John had been on the scene for only a short period of time but his impact was significant, even capturing the attention of religious leaders in Jerusalem. His dress, speech and lifestyle were similar to that of Elijah the prophet. John had a specific mission and his fiery, ascetic life captured the imagination of Israel, leading to large numbers coming to him for baptism. Zealous Jews, especially younger men, joined his movement and became his disciples. His primary mission was to prepare Israel for the Messiah by calling the people to repentance and baptizing them. He had specific advice about moral conduct and rules for living a life of holiness (Lk 3:1-20). He was committed to keeping the Law and he denounced sin in all of its forms. John's abrupt and blunt style repelled the Jewish religious leaders but stirred deeply the imagination of the masses.

The Disciples of Jesus

The third of these groups was Jesus and his disciples. This movement was very new, having only been on the scene for a few months. In some ways this was the most striking of the three movements because of its charismatic leader and the ambivalence felt by both insiders and outsiders toward his conduct. Jesus had a definite advantage over other groups because of his ability to perform spectacular feats of healing and his confrontation of powers. He was devoted to the Law and to Jewish religious practices but, at the same time, he appeared careless about his conduct and associated with people outside the bounds of orthodoxy. G. K. Chesterson described him as a man who "never lost his taste for bad company." Jesus was a change agent. Many of those close to his age and large numbers of women were attracted to him and became his followers.

The Two Divisions

Two of these groups are fasting and one is not. The problem that awakens this question is that Jesus and his disciples are not fasting while the other two groups are fasting. So, in terms of observable, external behavior these three groups are divided into the Pharisees and John on one side and Jesus on the other. John and the Pharisees are meeting an external righteousness expected of the devout while Jesus appears to be violating this standard. This fast Jesus is neglecting was probably a very important one, but it seems that the absence of fasting by Jesus and his disciples was becoming a known pattern. In other words, it was not just this one fast that Jesus was not observing, but the spiritual discipline of fasting was completely omitted by Jesus. The Pharisees and John were in agreement on the importance of fasting. How could Jesus neglect the discipline of fasting and still be considered a righteous person?

Three Illustrations

Jesus responds to this highly emotional issue by asking questions and giving three little stories. The three illustrations he uses are out of the daily life of the Jews. The first comes out of the Jewish marriage custom. This illustration is given specifically in answer to the question about fasting. The second and third illustrations come from agriculture and tailoring, having to do with winemaking and sewing.

Jewish marriage custom was highly ritualized and followed a well-known pattern. Marriage celebrations among Jews normally lasted for a week. Naturally a chief characteristic of these celebrations was that of joy. The bride and groom, along with the attendants, were exempt from normal religious practices, especially fasting. It was an occasion for eating, drinking and enjoying life. To refuse food and drink would be to insult the wedding couple and to mock the entire celebration.

The second and third illustrations give general principles that go well beyond the issue of fasting. Here Jesus gives a glimpse of his overall philosophy of ministry as it relates to the Jewish religious system. He illustrates this by saying that you would not cut a patch out of a new garment to patch an old garment. Second, when new wine is being made you do not put this wine in old wineskins. New wine must be poured into new wineskins.

Interpretation

This overview has given some feel for the socio-historical context of this episode and has hinted at some possible interpretations that will come out of this story. We now turn specifically to the task of interpretation with a keen interest in what this passage reveals about Jesus' agenda for change.

The Issues Under Consideration

What precisely are the issues being discussed in this passage? The first, and most obvious, is fasting. This is the issue that occasions the discussion. Fasting is a discipline associated with sorrow, suffering or need. A person abstains from food and sometimes liquid to focus on prayer. It is a crisis time. Although there was only one fast required of all Jews, the Day of Atonement, obviously there were many other occasions in a person's life that could lead to fasting. For the Pharisees, their concern for holiness had led them to give two days a week to fasting (Lk 18:12). It is also obvious from the context that fasting had become somewhat standardized in religious life and it was anticipated that all those who wanted to be holy would practice fasting.

The context also points to a specific occasion of fasting. The larger context of this question, included in each synoptic account, helps to understand the discussion even better. Prior to this question about fasting Jesus calls the tax collector Levi to join his inner group of disciples (5:27-32). In responding to Jesus' invitation Levi settles his affairs and throws a "great banquet" where he invites a large group of people, including a number of his tax collector buddies, along with Jesus. So, leading up to this question about fasting is Jesus' conduct. He has been partying with tax collectors, which had led the Pharisees to question him about this: "Why do you eat and drink with tax collectors and 'sinners'?" Jesus had responded to this question by saying, "It is not the healthy who need a doctor, but the sick."

Jesus responds to the accusation about his disciples not fasting by giving an illustration of a wedding. It is obvious that the bridegroom in this illustration is Jesus and the guests of the bridegroom are his disciples. One of the common metaphors of the future reign of God was that of a wedding banquet. Jesus is the Messiah and his time with his disciples is like a wedding. If Jesus is the Messiah, then the central characteristic of his presence is joy. It would be ludicrous to abstain from food and drink while the bridegroom was present. But Jesus does not stop here. He continues by saying that there will be a future time when fasting will be appropriate. A wedding cannot last forever. Eventually the bridegroom will be "taken from them" and when this happens they should fast. Many commentaries argue that this phrase suggests the bridegroom will be removed violently (Caird 1963:97; Marshall 1978:236).

The first illustration Jesus gives provides insight into the nature of Jesus' understanding of his calling. But it only deals with an external difference between himself and the Pharisees. In the second and third illustration Jesus moves below the surface to deal with the fundamental difference between himself and the Pharisees. Here Jesus throws down the challenge for change.

Luke's way of phrasing the issue of tailoring is distinct. Mark and Matthew state it this way: "No one sews a patch of unshrunk cloth on an old garment," while Luke states it this way: "No one tears a patch from a new garment and sews it on an old one." While both give the same idea about the relationship between new cloth and old, it is Luke's statement about tearing a patch from a new garment that is striking. In this illustration Jesus is not just comparing one item of religious practice, but is moving to a comparison of the whole. The new cloth represents the way of life introduced by Jesus and the old cloth represents the Pharisaic way of life. This illustration reveals a fundamental incompatibility between the Pharisaic religious system and the messianic movement. He is not saying that there is an incompatibility between the Jewish Scriptures and the messianic movement. Rather, his message challenges the basic tenets of first-century Pharisaic interpretation. Both are committed to God but their approach to God, the law and life are quite different. The message of Jesus calls for a paradigm shift.

The next illustration is even more vivid and suggestive concerning the difference between messianic faith and Judaism. In this illustration Jesus talks about wine (old and new) and wineskins (old and new). This new wine cannot be poured into the old wineskins. To attempt this will not only destroy the old wineskins but will result in a loss of the new wine. Perhaps the distinction made between form and function/meaning would be helpful in analyzing this illustration. Form refers to what can be seen, the external, while meaning refers to the essence (Hiebert 1985:29-58). For instance, most people when buying a car are interested in both form and meaning. Form refers to such things as styling, color and comfort. Meaning refers to such things as the performance of the car and the durability of the engine. Looking at Jesus' illustration this way could lead to the following interpretation:

Old wine = the Pharisaic religious system based on detailed interpretations of the Mosaic Law. This interpretation of the law had become authoritative for Pharisees and for many Jews who were not Pharisees.

Old wineskins = Numerous interpretations of the Mosaic Law on such things as eating, fasting, Sabbath observances with religious faith controlled by the priests and religious practice outlined by the Pharisees.

New wine = The new covenant based on the death of

Christ and the empowering of the Holy Spirit.

New wineskins = The new wineskins will flow out of the new Spirit-filled life. Certainly it will be decentralized and much more egalitarian than the previous system.

Jesus here introduces a new dimension to this whole question of how to live a righteous life. Jesus followed many of the external practices of Judaism, such as synagogue/ Temple attendance, wearing the robe of a teacher and preaching only to Jews. But as was noted in chapter two, he constantly pushed the boundaries of the major paradigm of his day, especially in the matter of relationships. His teaching was so powerful because he moved beyond external conduct to deal with issues of attitude and character. He also focused on the fundamentals of justice, compassion and worship of God. What are the fundamental principles outlined in these stories, and what insights can be gained from this passage for our life today?

Reflection/Application

What Does This Passage Reveal About Fasting?

Fasting does not have great prominence in Scripture, especially in the New Testament. But because it is a spiritual practice that challenges us in an area of basic human need it can be used to great benefit (Foster 1978:41-53). It also may be one of the most dangerous disciplines of the Christian life. Why do I say this? Fasting requires a person to deny themselves the fundamental biological need to eat. The most natural reaction to this practice is to expect that God will be pleased with our sacrifice and will respond by rewarding us. This attitude quickly draws us out of the realm of grace and turns the discipline into a practice of works. We abstain from food to merit God's favor.

Does Jesus' response to the questioners give any clues as to his understanding of this practice? Jesus clearly shows that the practice of fasting does have some place in a person's life. The fact that Jesus neither nor his disciples are fasting, along with his illustration of a wedding, should not be over-interpreted. Before launching his mission Jesus fasted forty days (Lk 4:1-11)! Also, Jesus says his disciples will fast in the future (v. 35). Thus a general answer to the question of what Jesus is teaching about fasting is this: There is a time to fast and there is a time to feast.

If, then, fasting is a legitimate discipline, does Jesus give any clue as to when it is appropriate to fast? And, does he also reveal when it is inappropriate to fast? The answer to both questions is yes. When, then, is it inappropriate to fast? The answer is found in Jesus' illustration. It is inappropriate to fast when the bridegroom is near. Jesus came as the bridegroom bringing joy and giving every reason to celebrate. Jesus came preaching the Good News and announcing that the kingdom of God was near. This was no time to fast. But, one may argue, Jesus is not here any longer and the wedding has ended. This is true only in a physical sense. The time of Jesus' mission was special and unique in an historical sense. But it is also true that the fundamental characteristic of the church and the kingdom is that of joy. The bridegroom is with us and much of our Christian life is one of joy and thrill at the nearness of the kingdom. The new wine of the Holy Spirit is present in our lives. It is inappropriate to fast when the bridegroom is near. The bridegroom's nearness calls for feasting.

When, then, is it appropriate to fast? Jesus tells his questioners (and his disciples) that one day the bridegroom will be taken from them and this would lead them to fasting. This refers to the death of Christ. While Luke does not talk about fasting on the part of the apostles at the death of Jesus, there is a principle laid down about fasting in this response. It is appropriate to fast when the bridegroom has been taken away. Although a keynote of Christianity is joy, another note that runs through the music of life is that of sorrow. There will be times when the bridegroom will be taken away. It may be a crisis of faith brought on by a tragic death, a broken relationship, a crisis of ministry or life, a period of isolation or even a time of doubting whether God cares and loves us. Heaven may seem like brass. Or, there could be some vision that God is calling us to and we desperately need an encouraging or affirming word from God. These are the occasions when it is appropriate to fast. Fasting for the Christian cannot be governed by the calender or tradition. Fasting is determined by the situations we encounter.

God's People Tend to Legalize and Externalize the Good News

The most natural tendency in the world is to routinize religious faith to the point of making it innocuous. Judaism had to become institutionalized to survive. For socialization to occur there must be the concretization of faith. When this occurs the next step is to measure reality by what can be ritualized and externalized. The Pharisees were God's people. This movement had developed out of the desperate desire of some of the Jews to prevent absorption into the Hellenized lifestyle. To avoid this problem the Pharisees called for a separation from Greek culture and the following of God's law. They began to outline in specific ways how God's people could follow God's laws. They developed guidelines on purification, Sabbath observance, spiritual disciplines and almost every aspect of life. Imperceptibly these guidelines for holiness became the standard by which they measured spirituality.

The language used by the gospel writers in talking about the relationship of the Pharisees and Jesus seems somewhat harsh and can lead Christians to have a distorted view of early Judaism. These records should not be over-interpreted. It should be read as a problem between two different Jewish groups who both loved God. But Jesus' lifestyle and faith called Israel back to the inner meaning of their faith. The Pharisees felt threatened and their challenge of Jesus led to increasing acrimony. This same kind of animosity can be seen between religious groups today.

This tendency to externalize and legalize can be seen throughout the history of the Christian church. For instance, when John Wesley had his conversion experience at a Moravian meeting in 1738 he was a priest and missionary in the Anglican Church. The Anglican Church tried to follow God's word and was very orthodox. When Wesley understood justification by faith he felt that he had been born again and his understanding, expression and practice of the Christian life changed radically. He went back into his church preaching this message with enthusiasm and warmth. His fellow priests were now offended by what he said and felt that he was too extreme. They eventually refused to let him preach in their churches. For the rest of his life they rejected his understanding of the Christian life and refused to let him participate as a preacher and brother in Anglican life (Tyson 1989:92-111).

The Basic Nature of the Gospel is Perpetual Newness

Wesley's life above all illustrates this principle. As the gospel is accepted, gradually, through the process of socialization, it becomes a part of the routine of life. But the Holy Spirit always calls God's people to revisit this newness. Sometimes this newness is discovered through a new way of looking at an old truth, or by rediscovering a truth that has been forgotten. For instance, during my first years as a missionary I discovered the reality and meaning of spiritual gifts. I eventually wrote a syllabus and taught on this subject throughout the churches in Trinidad and Tobago. This discovery led to a new understanding of the Holy Spirit and the vital importance of spiritual gifts in the practical life of the church. I gained a new appreciation of the importance of each member of the church. The church is a body and all parts of this body are equally important. I needed the ministry of every member of the body of Christ. In the past three decades, the rediscovery of the church as the body of Christ in which every member receives a spiritual gift and is called to use this gift has led to renewal for many Christians. Out of this discovery has come many new churches and the renewal of old churches with participation of all the members in the life of the church. Along with this is the renewed practice of meeting in small groups where each member can be loved, supported, affirmed, disciplined and rebuked.

Jesus' message of the kingdom of God brought renewal throughout the nation of Israel. Jews from the margins of society who had lost hope of pleasing God were awakened to new life through the compassion and tenderness of Jesus. Devout and simple Jews from the center of Jewish life, such as Peter and John and their families, found the promise and demand of Jesus' call to discipleship to be the answer to their deepest needs (Lk 5:1-11). This message of liberation cannot be completely submerged in spite of all of the various forms and rituals introduced in the church. Men and women, such as Bernard of Clairvaux, Francis of Assisi, Teresa of Avila and Martin Luther, are proof of the power of the message of Jesus and its ever renewing quality.

God Cannot Be Contained in Any of Our Forms

The creation of forms to express the meaning of faith is normal. The challenge is to distinguish between form and meaning and to recognize that the forms tend to become more important than the meaning. Recently a young Christian man came into a church I was attending and sat through the entire service with his hat on. Afterwards a couple of the older Christians made derogatory remarks about him. Why? Because we know that good Christians who want to please God do not wear hats in a service. Christian services are attended by normal people who sit in rows, do not participate in the service apart from the group activities of singing and giving and who sit quietly while a speaker stands up in front of them and gives a talk. All of those who attend these services sit on benches and wear normal clothes. Gradually forms become the standard for meaning.

A little over thirty years ago there were thousands of young people who started a hippie movement in California. Many of them dropped out of normal society and developed a countercultural lifestyle. This lifestyle included communalism, permissiveness, men growing long hair, wearing no shoes and for many of them the taking of drugs. After a few years there developed a growing interest in spirituality, but because of their lifestyle they were not welcomed in most churches. Yet in a little chapel in Costa Mesa a pastor named Chuck Smith invited these young people into his chapel. If they wished to sit on the floor he had no objections. When they got saved he simply taught them the gospel and baptized them in the ocean. Today Calvary Chapels are scattered across the world.

God is always breaking out with new forms that will release his power and life. The Pentecostal church provides another good illustration of the power of God being released in new forms. This movement which began at the turn of the century now numbers more than 200 million members around the world (Synan 1992:10). Pentecostal Christianity has sometimes been referred to as the "third ecclesiology" because its forms of worship are so sharply distinguished from Catholicism and Protestantism. At first spurned and reviled by traditional Christianity, today there is a growing recognition that God simply poured out his new wine into new wineskins when he created Pentecostalism.

The Most Natural Response to Change is Resistance

This response is natural because change creates tension in our life and not all change is constructive. But at the same time the resistance to change can result in death, physically and spiritually. Many of the changes in our society, especially in the area of value changes, must be resisted by Christians. Surveys indicate that a majority of our society is pro-choice on the issue of abortion. For the Christian who believes that abortion is the killing of life this change must be resisted.

But, based on this passage as well as the nature of the gospel, every Christian must be continuously open to the desire of the Holy Spirit to change us and enable us to experience the new wine. The story of William Cameron

Townsend illustrates this need. As a young man doing colporteur work in Central America he regularly met people who could not read the Spanish language. This awakened him to the need of Bible translation. When he approached his mission about this need they were not open to changing the direction of the mission. This led him to the founding of a new mission, which he named Summer Institute of Linguistics. God poured out his Spirit on this work.

Change Illustrated from Acts

How does the story of the wine and wineskins work itself out in the early history of this movement? Luke's second volume tells how this new messianic movement met the challenge of change and became a worldwide movement. In the opening of his narrative Luke shows this movement growing rapidly while experiencing some tension with Jewish religious leaders (Ac 1–5). It starts out completely Jewish and shows no signs of trying to reach non-Jews. This idyllic picture of the Jesus movement Luke has painted in the first five chapters is broken in chapter six by an unexpected crisis. This crisis results in a change in the direction of this movement as it is swept up into a maelstrom of God's purpose that does not end until the leadership from Gentile and Jewish churches has self-consciously identified its nature and purpose as universal. This process of moving from a renewal movement within Judaism to a distinctly separate movement that has abandoned historic particularism is a complicated record of radical religious and social changes.

What are the changes this movement had to go through in moving from the particular to the universal? A summary of the changes will be given by looking at four broad areas of change. The summary will focus on the cultic, geographical, ethnic and relational dimensions of this change.

Cultic Dimensions

Israel's cultic life was unique to its own history and faith. Messianic faith faced serious cultic implications as it

moved from particularism to universalism. While Luke gives
few specific details about the cultic changes that took place
as Gentiles became Christians, radical changes were taking
place during these first thirty years. Specific awareness of
the change introduced by this new message comes when the
Jews bring accusations against Stephen in 6:11-14. They accuse him of speaking against the Temple and the custom of
Moses, implying some relationship between Jesus, the center
of messianic worship, and the cultus. Perhaps Stephen was
hinting that the cultic aspects of Judaism would have to be
abandoned by those who were committed to Jesus Christ.
But there are indications that Jewish believers continued
many of the practices related to the Temple. In fact, it cannot
be stated with certainty that the Jewish believers terminated
any of their traditional cultic observances of Judaism after
joining the messianic movement.

Did they, for instance, cease offering sacrifices in the
Temple? Luke does not touch on this subject. Throughout
Acts Jewish Christians continued to be circumcised and keep
the Mosaic law. According to Luke, Paul can circumcise bor-
derline Jews, observe Nazarite vows and join in purification
rites in the Temple while walking arm in arm around Jerusalem with his Gentile converts (16:3; 18:19; 21:27). On the
other hand it can be stated categorically that Gentiles were
released from all the cultic aspects of Judaism. Luke makes
this very clear in Acts 15. Here the church agreed that the
traditional requirement of circumcision implied a commitment to all aspects of the Mosaic law, including the cultic
requirements. Gentiles are no longer obligated to be circumcised and are released from all cultic obligations. Circumcision is declared soteriologically insignificant (15:8-11). So,
although Luke's narrative shows little interest in dealing
with specific cultic changes involved in this movement becoming universal, at the same time he provides information
that implies a radical change taking place in the economy of
salvation history. If Gentiles can become good Christians
and enter into full fellowship with Jewish Christians without
observing the cultic rituals, then these observances have lost
their soteriological significance.

Geographical Dimensions

Luke's entire record of the messianic movement confines it geographically to Palestine until Acts 9. In Acts 6 Luke introduces the Hellenists as transitional influences, hinting at the geographical changes coming. Then, with the ministry of Philip in chapter 8, the reader is taken into the province of Samaria and then south of Jerusalem along the Gaza road where a person from the geographical borders of the world becomes a believer. After this the conversion of the ringleader of those persecuting the church takes place in the Gentile city of Damascus. The paradigmatic story of Peter's ministry to Cornelius takes place in the city built by Herod the Great to be the center of Roman government in Palestine. Immediately after this account Luke follows the gospel as it penetrates Antioch, a pagan city of international importance and the center of East-West confluence, some 300 miles from Jerusalem. The gospel's geographical extension in Acts 6–15 concludes with the travels of Paul in the Roman provinces of Cyprus, Pamphylia and South Galatia. Paul travels deeper and deeper into the Roman world, then returns to Jerusalem, where, through the attack of the Jews, he eventually reaches Rome, witnessing to "all" who came to him.

Christianity was established in major Roman cities, impacting Caesarea, Antioch and Ephesus. It was impacting the mainstream of life in major Greco-Roman cities. Just as the Jewish faith changed through the influence of diaspora Jews, so Christianity will change as it extends geographically. The geographical spread of the movement was proof that its message was acceptable to both people of power and influence and to ordinary people in the major cities of the Roman Empire.

Ethnic Dimensions

By the time Luke's story has reached the Jerusalem Council in Acts 15, Samaritans, an Ethiopian eunuch, a Roman soldier and assorted Gentiles have become members of this messianic movement *without changing their culture.* Ethnic universalism becomes an historical reality by the time of this council. The ethnic makeup of this movement signals the revolutionary changes that have occurred in these two decades.

The first major cross-cultural encounter of this movement can be found in the subcultural differences among Jewish Christians. Luke's focus on the Hellenists, Stephen and Philip, indicate that their understanding of the Christian message was strikingly different at some points.

And what about the Samaritans? When this new movement incorporates Samaritans, this signals a major change, distinguishing it sharply from historic Judaism. Very soon the Samaritans are followed by an Ethopian eunuch, a Gentile God-fearer and eventually Gentiles out in the diaspora. Finally, the Jerusalem Council makes a theological commitment to all that has occurred. Paul's further evangelistic ministry does not modify this picture in any significant way. Even though the cultural differences between Jews and Gentiles are not specified, the reader is left with little doubt that major cultural thresholds have been crossed at the end of Luke's narrative. The gospel has arrived in Rome and Paul preaches to all who come to him.

Relational Dimensions

In the relationship between Jews and Gentiles within the Christian context, Luke reveals the most specific information about changes experienced by the Jewish church. There are at least three passages that deal with Jews and Gentiles eating together. These three instances (Ac 10-11, 15 and 16:33) show specifically the implications for Jews and only the decree of Acts 15 contains the implication for Gentiles. A study of the dietary laws given to the Jews and the history of how they carried out these laws shows the strategic place, cross-culturally, that table-fellowship played in the preservation of their particularity.

Anthropologists and sociologists have demonstrated that the divisions of animals and people in Israel's religion were interrelated (Douglas 1982b; Malina 1981). Further, the division of people within Israel was based on their proximity, from a purity standpoint, to the Temple, with priests being the closest and Gentiles being the most distant. So, what a person ate was vitally related to the issue of holiness as there was a relationship between the kind of food one ate and its appropriateness for the altar. In other words the cultic life of the Israelite was replicated in his rules for eating. These insights help the modern reader understand the commitment of Jews to maintaining the boundaries among themselves and between themselves and Gentiles. While the contingencies of history forced them into the closest possible relationship to Gentiles, making ritual purity increasingly difficult to maintain, ordinary Jews did not abandoned these guidelines. The two main areas where these boundaries were clear and had to be maintained were in marriage and eating. Luke's narrative deals only with the issue of table-fellowship between Jews and Gentiles.

Conclusion

Within three short decades this orthodox Jewish movement founded by Jesus of Nazareth has undergone radical cultic, ethnic, geographical and relational changes. The principles for the change can be found throughout Jesus' ministry but are conceptualized in his very brief response to his questioners about the issue of fasting (Lk 5:33-39). The good news, like new wine, must be poured into new wineskins. The gospel calls the church and individual Christians to constant renewal. The history of the church is the history of the tension between renewal and transformation and the stubborn refusal to change, regarding forms as more important than meaning.

Personal Response and Reflection

1. List the three Jewish groups in Luke 5:33-39 and tell how each one sought to bring about change.

2. State in your own words when it is appropriate to fast. When have you found it important to fast in your own experience?

3. Are there tendencies toward legalism in your own church tradition? What are some of the dangers toward legalism in your own life?

4. What changes are you currently seeing in society right now that will require changes for individual Christians and the church in the immediate future?

PART 2

Gentile Mission: Process

For two thousand years God had been working out his will within one particular ethnic group. While Gentiles from many ethnic and cultural backgrounds were free to join the people of God, they had to leave their own people and become members of the Jewish people (Ru 1:16-17). This change was not just religious but also cultural. They were socialized into Jewishness. How can a movement within Judaism, however radical, reach out to other cultural groups and share the Good News without also requiring them to become Jewish? Is it possible for good Jews, such as Peter, to preach to Gentiles and allow them to remain uncircumcised while becoming Christians?

Luke, while implying the universalism of Jesus' message throughout volume one, shows the Jesus Movement, begun by Jesus of Nazareth and continued by the "disciples whom he chose" (Ac 1:2), retaining its particularism until chapter 6 of his second volume. Then in incremental fashion the author shows how this message became culturally universal. Although the messianic movement has been characterized by particularism up to this point, Luke shows that God has been laying a foundation for its eventual universalization. This preparation took the form of prophetic allusions (Lk 3:6), messianic proclamation (Lk 4:16-37), ministry intimations (Lk 15:1), and programmatic outline (Ac 1:8).

A primary purpose of Luke's narrative is to unfold for his reader the story of how Gentiles came to be included with Jews as part of the people of God. Luke signals a decisive change taking place in the direction of this movement in Acts 6. This decisive change arrives at some level of conceptual culmination in Acts 15 when the church stops to reflect on what has been happening. After intense debate and discussion, the leadership of this movement self-consciously affirms and thoughtfully declares that the message they are preaching is universally applicable. It is equally valid for Jews as Jews and Gentiles as Gentiles. Luke records Peter saying: "We believe it is through the grace of our Lord Jesus that we [Jews] are saved, just as they [Gentiles] are" (15:11).

This is a missionary story par excellence. It is naturally assumed by modern readers that any missionary story will involve a cross-cultural dimension. To say that the gospel moves from one ethnic group to another is to declare that there are cultural issues involved in this process. Luke is the only writer within the first century to write anything like a history of the Christian movement telling how different cultural groups embraced the gospel. While Paul states the universalization of the gospel as a fact, Luke alone gives in narrative form the progressive steps involved in the gospel moving from a purely Jewish context to a universal context.

Does Luke have theological intentions to indicate some of the cultural changes, tensions, conflicts and adaptations involved in this process? Or does Luke's focus on the theological dimensions of the story automatically exclude any interest he might have in the cross-cultural nature of this process? It will be seen that Luke's narrative approach in recounting this movement makes it somewhat difficult at times to discover the sociological dynamics of the process. But because his theological intentions are recorded with significant historical socio-cultural data, these data provide information for cross-cultural reflection.

The structure of Luke's narrative is highly schematic, especially from chapter 6 through 15. He deliberately chooses events in the early story of the messianic movement that show how God moved the gospel step by step from Jewish particularism to universalism. Each episode in these chapters, with the exception of chapter 12, advances this movement in the direction of universalism until the church leadership explicitly announces the completion of this process in chapter 15.

This section will contain three chapters that focus on some of the major steps in the gospel becoming universal. There will be no attempt to discuss all of the details of these chapters; special attention will be given to Acts 6:1-7; 8:1-40; 9:32-11:18 and 15:1-21, with brief references to the sections in between. The first chapter in this section will show how the Hellenists influenced major changes in the direction of the Jesus movement. Peter's ministry to Cornelius, involving not only the conversion of this Gentile and his family, but also the radical enlargement of Peter's understanding of the universal implications of the gospel, will be discussed in chapter 5. With a growing number of Gentiles becoming Christians without circumcision, a church council is convened in Jerusalem. Chapter 6 will show how this council, made up of representatives from the Jewish and Gentile churches, confirms universalism as God's will.

4

The Hellenists: Bridging People

Questions to Consider before
Reading this Chapter

*Challenge: Your church is ethnically particular in an ethnically diverse community. You have been asked by your church leaders to participate in a discussion group on how they can reach out to the other cultural groups in the community. How do you think this can best be done in your church? Where would you begin?

*Read rapidly Acts six through eight. Why do you think Luke chooses to bring the Seven, Stephen and Philip to the center of his story at this point rather than continue his story around the apostles?

For the past twelve years I have lived in Whittier, California. During this short period of time, this city of 110,000 has moved from a dominantly Anglo city to an Anglo minority. In recent years I have spoken in some of the Anglo churches. I notice that most of them continue to be dominantly Anglo. But there are some exceptions. Those that are exceptions have some common ingredients. Those churches that look more like the city in ethnicity have pastors that feel comfortable around different cultural groups and make these people feel welcome. But, perhaps even more important, these pastors give some visibility to the ethnic diversity of the church. They look for those who relate well to the Anglo culture and the non-Anglo culture and give them responsibility within the church. For instance, in one Anglo church the pastor encourages new non-Anglo members to assume ministries, such as ushering. Ushers are often the first people that visitors meet when entering the church. I refer to those who are comfortable with different cultures as bridging people. Without bridging people in key, visible positions in the church, most churches in cities with changing demographics will dwindle away and die. This same principle can be seen in the early church.

In chapters 1 through 5 Luke records how the tiny Jesus movement took root within Jerusalem through the leadership of the apostles and especially the prominence of Peter, eventually becoming a large and powerful movement (2:41; 4:4; 5:12-16). This growth begins with the coming of the Holy Spirit (2:1ff) and quickly penetrates all of Jerusalem. Through preaching and performance of signs and wonders it becomes a powerful minority movement within Judaism in a matter of a couple of years. While this movement has experienced at least one internal problem and some persecution from the Sanhedrin during the first five chapters, Luke's record accents the unity, oneness and mutual sharing that characterized the messianic community (2:42-47; 4:32-37; 5:1-11; 5:17ff.). Luke uses phrases such as, "all the believers were one in heart and mind" (4:32); "no one claimed that any of his possessions was his own, but they shared everything they had" (4:33); and "there was no needy person among them" (4:34a), to describe this new movement.

It is therefore something of a shock to discover in chapter 6 a problem that threatens to split this young movement. The atmosphere of unity Luke's narrative has created is quickly dispelled, both by internal and external pressures. The rapid growth of this movement is due in part to the large influx of Hellenist Jews. The Hellenists play a key role in the universalization of Christianity. Luke's section on the Hellenists—6:1 to 8:40—divides naturally into three parts: first, there is an account of the first organization of the church (6:1-7); second, Luke tells of Stephen's ministry and martyrdom (6:8 to 8:3); and third, he records the ministry of Philip.

Hebrews and Hellenists—6:1-7

Acts 6 provides the starting point in discussing some of the major differences manifested in early Christianity. One's interpretation of this passage will influence one's entire picture of Christianity during the first century. There have been some major contributions made by Lukan scholars on the subject of the Hellenists (Cadbury 1979: 59-73; Hengel 1979: 71-80, 1983:1-29, 48-64; Jervell 1983:13-51; Moule 1959:100-102).

Verse one opens with Luke introducing the "Grecian Jews" and "Hebraic Jews" as two significant divisions within this new messianic movement. There is also an interesting switch in this section from a focus on the apostles to the Hellenists. In fact the apostles are rather abruptly pulled off the stage at this point. Although the apostles will continue to play a vital role in Luke's story they will gradually move into the shadows and disappear completely (9:26ff., 9:32-11:18; 12:1-25; 15:1-35) after 16:4. Acts 6:1-7 records the first major church problem encountered in this young movement and how the issue was resolved so as to maintain the unity and continued growth of the church. The problem seems to arise over improper food distribution. The "Grecian Jews [were complaining] against the Hebraic Jews because their widows were being overlooked in the daily distribution of food" (6:1). At the suggestion of the Twelve the disciples choose seven men to handle this daily distribution. The apostles affirm the Seven and the church continues to grow and expand, even attracting a "great many of the priests" (v. 7).

What place does this very brief episode play in Luke's story of the Christian movement? Luke accomplishes three objectives in this paragraph.

The Hellenists Are Brought on the Stage

Luke's primary intention here is not to discuss the church problem that arises but rather to introduce his readers to the Hellenists (Marshall 1980:124ff.). This is confirmed by the very brief space given to the problem (seven verses on this church problem contrasted with seventy-one verses on Stephen). Luke records how this Messianic movement, beginning in Jerusalem within the Jewish religious system, breaks the historic hold of particularism and becomes a worldwide movement. The Hellenists play a crucial role in the church and by recounting the food problem Luke finds a natural way to introduce the Hellenists.

His first mention of the Hellenists occurs in verse one. Apparently they are already a significant force within the congregation. Luke could have introduced the Hellenists earlier in his narrative. For instance, Barnabas (4:36-37) was probably a Hellenist. From Barnabas' generous act of a large donation, along with subsequent history where the church raises funds for Jerusalem (Ac 11:27ff.; 2 Cor. 8–9) it could be inferred that the Hellenist Christians were the major financial supporters of this messianic movement.

Hellenist leaders are introduced when the Seven are chosen to assist the Twelve in handling the material needs of the movement (v. 5). All of the Seven have Greek names, probably, but not conclusively, indicating that all are Hellenists (Conzelmann 1987:45). Although Stephen dominates Luke's narrative from 6:8 through 8:3, other Hellenists, such as Philip and the unknown disciples of Acts 11:19, continue this

movement after the martyrdom of Stephen. Luke also intends to link Paul and Barnabas, at least partially, with this
Hellenist movement (4:36-37; 9:26-29). If Paul is linked to the
Hellenists then much of the credit for the mission to the Gentiles can be attributed to them (Johnson 1977:211ff.).

Luke's style is to gradually introduce his readers to his
main characters before they become prominent in his story.
This can be demonstrated with his major characters, such as
Jesus, Peter and Paul (Lk 1:5-2:1; 5:1-10; Ac 7:58-8:3), and
with his minor characters, such as Stephen, Philip and Barnabas (Ac 6:1-6; 4:36-37). Luke very obliquely brings Stephen
into his narrative in Acts 6:5. While Stephen is not the center
of this section (vv. 1-7), he is given a prominence that makes
him stand out among the Seven. Luke specifically describes
Stephen as a man "full of faith and of the Holy Spirit" (v. 5).

Diversity is Introduced

The first five chapters of Acts gives the impression that
this Jesus movement consisted exclusively of homogeneous
Jews. But with his opening sentence of chapter 6 Luke
abruptly introduces the reader to some kind of diversity
within the movement. The inadequate distribution of food is
not indiscriminate but is evenly divided along socio-cultural
and/or linguistic lines (Marshall 1980:124-28). While there is
general agreement among Lukan scholars that these two
terms, Grecian Jews and Hebraic Jews, indicate some kind of
cultural difference, there is not complete agreement on what
this difference is. Cadbury says that most scholars interpret
these two terms as an indication of Greek-speaking Jews, i.e.,
diaspora Jews whose first language was Greek, and Palestinian Jews, i.e., Jews whose primary language was Aramaic (1979:59-73).

Hengel's recent studies of this passage leads him to conclude that the traditional interpretation continues to be the
most convincing (Hengel 1983:2-25). The word *Hellenistas* occurs three times (6:1; 9:29; 11:19) in Acts and cannot be found
in any other source before the time of Chrysostom in the

fourth century (Haenchen 1971:260). Second, Luke's first un-debated use of the word Greeks (*Hellenas*) is in Acts 14:1 in the context of the synagogue and is used as the opposite of Jews. This reference, along with its appearance in Acts 21:28 indicates a distinction between Greeks and Hellenists (Hen-gel 1983:9). Third, the most natural interpretation of the only two unquestionable appearances of this word (Ac 6:1 and 9:29), where it occurs in a Jewish context, point in the direc-tion of some kind of qualifying description of Jews. Finally, Luke's very schematic presentation would make it highly unlikely that he would introduce Gentiles at this point in his story (Hengel 1983:8; cp. Cadbury 1979:65ff.). This would make Peter's ministry to Cornelius anti-climatic. Therefore, these Grecian Jews should be viewed as diaspora Jews who speak Greek.

Cultural Differences

By introducing the Hellenists Luke has implied a meas-ure of cultural difference within the Christian movement. He says that it is the *Hellenist* widows who are complaining that the *Hebrews* are getting all of the food. What is the cul-tural difference Luke is introducing? Many scholars believe that the difference was linguistic and cultural but not ethnic. It is usually assumed that the primary language of the Hel-lenists was Greek with some bilingualism and the primary language of the Hebrews was Aramaic with some also speaking Greek (Moule 1959:100-102).

Implications Based on Cultural Differences

If the linguistic and cultural difference are accepted then a number of observations could be made about both the oc-casion of the problem regarding food distribution and the persecution that arises against this movement. For instance, the reason the apostles could neglect the Hellenists would be explained by the church consisting of two worshipping, functioning groups, each group distinguished by a common heart language that allows each to express fully and freely their worship of God. The apostles, speaking primarily Aramaic, would have much less contact with the Hellenists. This would explain how they could neglect the Hellenist widows (Ac 6:2-3). It would also explain why Luke refers to the apostles as the "Twelve" because he is contrasting them with the "Seven." If the Hellenists were indeed worshipping in a separate group because of linguistic differences then it would be natural for leadership to develop within their own group. The Seven then would represent leaders who were already functional leaders within the Hellenists (vv. 2, 3). This would also explain why all of the seven have Greek names. They are, in fact, not only to handle the finances (suggesting power, influence, prestige) but they also are to be the spiritual leaders of the Hellenists. How else can one explain Luke's incidental reference to Philip as "one of the Seven" some twenty-five years after this incident (21:8)? If he was only a "deacon," then it is highly unlikely that this phrase would have been an appropriate title for him after such a long time (6:5, 21:8).

This interpretation would also explain the very enigmatic statement in 8:1 that all of the church was scattered out of Jerusalem after the death of Stephen "except the apostles." Luke certainly cannot want his readers to conclude that the only Christians left in Jerusalem were the apostles. Every subsequent glimpse of Jerusalem finds a functioning church in Jerusalem and only a decade later the apostles have been completely relieved of leadership roles in Jerusalem. Luke intends to say that it was primarily the Hellenists who were forced out of Jerusalem (9:26ff.; 11:22, 30). Confirmation of this interpretation can be found in the prominent place Hellenists occupy when he follows the spread of the gospel outside of Jerusalem (8:4ff.; 9:1ff.; 11:19ff.).

These cultural differences would also lead to differing theological viewpoints on the implications of Christ's death and resurrection. Perhaps the Hellenists, as had to happen sooner or later, were beginning to ask questions about the relationship between their Messianic faith and the Law; be-

tween Jesus Christ and the Temple; and between their faith
and the needs of the world (Meyer 1986:67-83). If this is accepted, then Stephen's message was missiological in nature.
If God is not limited to Jerusalem, then he can work anywhere in the diaspora. This would explain, then, why the
apostles seem to melt into the background and all of the persecution falls on the Hellenists. This is not to say that the
message of the Hebrews was not controversial. They experienced opposition but it was an opposition primarily from
the Sadducees with the Pharisees and the people being either
somewhat sympathetic or in some cases very supportive
(2:47; 5:17ff). Stephen's message brings down the wrath of
the whole nation on the Hellenists, including other Hellenists, the general population of Jews, the Sanhedrin and the
Pharisees (6:8, 12, 15; 7:58; 8:1-3). This indicates that Stephen
and the Hellenists were saying things that not only focused
on Jesus but implied that commitment to Jesus called for a
re-evaluation of the religious traditions represented by the
Mosaic law and the Temple (Meyer 1986).

A Word of Caution

Even when it is clear that the Seven all have Greek
names, this is not conclusive proof in itself that they were all
necessarily from the diaspora. After all, two of the apostles,
Philip and Andrew, have Greek names (Cadbury 1979:61-
62). There is an ongoing search for more precise information
on how extensively Greek language and culture had pen-
etrated Palestine during the early first century (Overman
1988:160-168). There is a growing belief on the part of some
scholars that Greek influence in Palestine was much greater
than previously thought and that a sizable minority of the
population had some level of fluency in the Greek language.
Further research on first century Palestine may show that the
Hebrews were more nearly bilingual than were the Hellenists:

There are many ossuary inscriptions from Palestine,
two thirds in Greek alone, one tenth in Greek and

Hebrew (or Aramaic). Since sepulchral inscriptions probably best indicate the language of the common people, it is significant that the vast majority of those published are in Greek. . . . Many scholars today conclude that Greek was widely used in first-century Palestine by Christians as well as other Jews. Whether more Greek or Aramaic was spoken in Palestine is debated (Stambaugh and Balch 1987:87).

The Ministry of Stephen—Acts 6:8–8:3

The martyrdom of Stephen marks a turning point in Luke's story and almost everything that happens from chapter 8 to 15 can be traced back to his death (8:4ff., 9:1ff., 11:18ff.). Luke's narrative of Stephen can be divided into three sections. In the first section he continues his introduction of Stephen by focusing on his ministry in the Hellenist synagogues in Jerusalem and the conflict that flows out of the synagogues into the street, eventually being taken up by the Sanhedrin (6:8-15). This very brief background is followed by Stephen's speech, which is the longest recorded speech by Luke in the entire book of Acts (7:1-50). Luke then concludes with an account of the martyrdom of Stephen (7:51-8:3).

The Charges Against Stephen

One cannot determine what exactly Stephen was saying about the Temple and the Mosaic law. While his accusers say that he is speaking against the Law, the Temple and the custom of Moses, Luke says that these charges came from "false witnesses" (6:13). This could mean that Luke is saying that there is no truth in their accusations, or, more likely, the way they express their accusations distorts what Stephen was actually saying (Wilson 1973:130ff.; cp Jervell 1972:145-46).

Stephen's Sermon

Stephen's sermon can be roughly divided into two broad sections: 7:1-43 and 7:44-50. The first section contains a brief survey of Jewish history that focuses exclusively on Abraham, Joseph and Moses. One thing that these three biblical patriarchs have in common is that God spoke to them outside of Palestine. God called Abraham out of pagan Mesopotamia, saved Israel through Joseph who was in Egypt, and gave the law to Moses in the wilderness. These three spent all, or most, of their life outside of Palestine. The focus is on God's revelational activity outside of the land. Almost all of what is recorded in this section places emphasis on the experience of the patriarchs in Gentile territory. If this choice of history is geographically specific, then it would point to an attack by Stephen on the exclusive claims of Palestinian Jews. In this way the Hellenists would be challenging the exclusivity of Jerusalem and the Temple.

The second section, 7:44-50, can be more readily connected with the accusations against Stephen. In this section Stephen draws some sharp contrasts between the tabernacle and the Temple. The text says that the tabernacle was "made as God directed" and that the builders followed the "pattern" given by God (v. 44). The following contrasts are made in the conclusion of this sermon: Solomon is contrasted with David; the divine is contrasted with the human; the adverb "however" indicates a contrast; and, finally, the quotation from Isaiah 66:1-2 indicates that the tabernacle was in some ways superior to the Temple.

Luke is trying to bring perspective on the relative importance of the Temple as there was always a tendency in Israel's history to absolutize the Temple. This can be seen at a number of places in the Old Testament, and the prophets were especially fond of relativizing its place in the life of Israel (Jer 1–20; Eze 10:1ff). A second explanation is that Luke is not primarily concerned about the Temple but about the character of God. He does not simply make relative the Temple; he contrasts it with the tabernacle in order to indicate the universality of God. God does not limit himself to any one place, even the Temple in Jerusalem. The tabernacle with its mobility communicates God's character of universalism.

The Martyrdom of Stephen

Stephen's martyrdom occurs quickly and Luke presents it in all of its brutality. Although Paul is present when Stephen is martyred, it is Luke alone who tells of Stephen's death. But Stephen is not the only church leader killed by the Sanhedrin during the first century. According to the Jewish historian Josephus (*Jewish Antiquities* 20:9), James, the brother of Jesus, is put to death through the instigation of the high priest Ananus some three decades later. It occurred during a transition in Roman government. When the new governor, Albinus, arrived in Jerusalem and learned of this illegal act, he relieved the high priest Ananus. Thus, precipitous and illegal action on the part of Jewish leaders was not unprecedented.

Stephen's death provides Luke an opportunity to introduce his readers to Saul, who is pictured as a participant who holds the clothes of those who stone Stephen (7:58). This ruthless action by the Jewish leaders culminating in Stephen's death is followed by such violent action that all of the Christians "except the apostles" are forced out of Jerusalem (7:58, 8:1ff.). Saul assumes active leadership in this persecution. This violent act on the part of the Sanhedrin concludes Luke's continuous narrative of the messianic movement in Jerusalem. This reform movement from rural Galilee, in seeking to bring reformation to the Jewish people, becomes, through the influence of the Hellenists, an empire-wide movement.

The Ministry of Philip—Acts 8:4–40

Luke next recounts the ministry of Philip the Hellenist, who first goes to the Samaritans (vv. 4-25), then to an Ethiopian (vv. 26-40). Philip, one of the Seven and an evangelist (21:8), becomes the first believer in Luke's narrative to extend the Christian movement outside of Jerusalem and into another people group (1:8).

Samaritans Become Christians

Luke has prepared his readers in a number of ways for this ministry among the Samaritans. In volume one Luke presents Samaritans as examples of charity and compassion and also uses them to reveal the unthankfulness and heartlessness of the Jewish religious leaders (10:35-37; 17:11-19). To Luke Samaritans are neither Jews nor Gentiles but a third category. They represent those who have betrayed the covenant yet seek to maintain their identity as the people of God. But to the Jews, Samaritans are even more despicable than the Gentiles.

There has been a growing scholarly interest both in the Samaritans and in Samaritan Christianity (Scobie 1973: 390-414; Coggins 1982:423-34). Luke's interest in the Samaritans as the first "non-Jews" to hear the good news and respond to it indicates their importance (1:8; 8:4ff.). A. J. Coggins says that "Samaritanism in the first century A.D. was a widespread and flourishing phenomenon" (1982:432). Their belief system approximated that of Judaism, but there were some notable distinctions between these two groups. One difference was the commitment of the Samaritans to Mt. Gerizim as opposed to Jerusalem on the part of the Jews. While both Jews and Samaritans had messianic beliefs, they were sharply divided on the nature of the messiah (Brown 1966:166-98). The Samaritans appear rather often in Josephus' history and there is little doubt about how he feels about them as is indicated in this quotation:

They alter their attitude according to circumstances, and when they see the Jews prospering, call them their kinsmen, on the ground that they are descended from Joseph, and are related to them through their origin from him, but, when they see the Jews in trouble, they say that they have nothing whatsoever in common, nor do these have any claims of friendship or race, but they declare themselves to be aliens of another race (*Antiquities* 9:14:3) (Whiston 1987).

Luke himself gives no indication of the kind of Christianity that developed out of Philip's ministry among the Samaritans or precisely what they believed prior to his arrival, even though he holds them up as examples of piety in his first volume. His account in Acts shows them to be exceptionally responsive when Philip preaches to them. When Philip preaches a messianic message to them they believe and are baptized (vv. 5, 12). Although they become Christians, they are hindered from full participation in the gospel until Peter and John arrive from Jerusalem.

Philip and the Eunuch—Acts 8:26-40

After briefly narrating the entrance of the Samaritans into the messianic movement, Luke tells of the further progress of the gospel through the conversion of a person who is ethnically and geographically distant from Jewish particularism. The eunuch is a person from a rather remote part of the earth (1:8). He is converted through the ministry of Philip and continues on his way back to Africa.

The sharp contrast drawn between this story and the previous one should be noted. In the account of the Samaritans, Luke's record indicates that it is Philip, who, having been driven out of Jerusalem, takes the initiative to go to the Samaritans and preach to them. In Philip's ministry to the Ethiopian, on the other hand, God initiates everything that happens. First an "angel of the Lord" guides Philip to the man. When Philip sees the man, the Spirit commands him to go near the chariot. Remarkably, when he draws near the chariot, he hears the man reading from Isaiah 53. When Philip finishes preaching, the eunuch, not Philip, suggests baptism. After Philip baptizes the eunuch he simply disappears from the Ethiopian's sight. While, then, Philip is an active participant in the first episode, he is passively active throughout this second narrative. He takes little initiative in evangelizing this man. It is God who takes the initiative.

The conversion of the Ethiopian will be the first of three conversion accounts that Luke gives, with each immediately succeeding the other. The other two are Saul (9:1-31) and Cornelius (9:32-11:18). But only the first two involve individual conversions, exclusively, as there is an entire household converted along with Cornelius in chapter 10. Each of these stories advances Luke's narrative of the universal dimensions of the gospel.

But exactly who is this Ethiopian? Since he is called an Ethiopian this would point to his non-Jewish origins. Gaventa has this to say about him:

> Luke first describes the person whom Philip sees as a male Ethiopian. That he is an Ethiopian would in itself arouse considerable interest on the part of Luke's audience. In the Greco-Roman world the term "Ethiopian" was applied to anyone who was dark-skinned, but especially to those who came from lands south of Egypt. Moreover, Greek writers showed considerable interest in Ethiopians. . . . Strabo's description of the Ethiopians, written not many decades prior to Luke-Acts, remarks that they came from the "extremities of the inhabited world" . . . in the Old Testament and in the writings of the church fathers, the Ethiopian is one who comes from the borders of the known world (Gaventa 1986:103)

Some contend that this man is a typical or symbolic convert. Another interpretation regards him as a proselyte because he has been to Jerusalem and is reading the Scriptures. It is difficult to say with certainty how this Ethiopian functions in Luke's overall narrative. The minimum that can be said, based on the flow of Luke's narrative, is that he is definitely not part of traditional Judaism as he almost certainly represents some broadening of the Jesus movement. But to regard him as a Gentile would preempt the place of Cornelius in Luke's narrative.

Reflections on the Cross-cultural Nature of Philip's Ministry

If Luke is writing schematically to show how the gospel moves from the particular to the universal, what place does the ministry of Philip play in this narrative? Do these two case studies reveal any intention on Luke's part to move the gospel, however incrementally, further away from Jewishness toward a greater degree of universalism? And, more importantly, does Luke intend to draw out the cross-cultural dimensions of the gospel as it moves out of a purely Jewish context?

The Samaritans

There have been a number of attempts to prove that for Luke these Samaritans would be classified as Jews. Some of Marshall's discussion seems to indicate that the Samaritans are to be distinguished from both Jews and Gentiles. In his discussion of Acts 8 he calls them schismatics. His further comments make it clear that he thinks of them as Jews when he says: "Although we might be tempted to see in the mission to Samaria the church's first attempt to evangelize Gentiles, this would be a wrong interpretation. . . . [they are] part of the lost sheep of the house of Israel" (1980:153). Jervell is also of the opinion that most New Testament scholars "regard the Samaritans as Gentiles" (1972:117). His statement is made with the presupposition that Samaritans must be either Jews or Gentiles. But Ellis, for instance, in his comments on Luke 17:11-19 says that the Samaritans are non-Jews (1966:209).

Luke's use of the term *foreigner* in Luke 17:18 needs to be noted. Bietenhard says: "*allogenes* occurs only in Luke 17:18.

The grateful Samaritan who returned to give thanks after being healed of his leprosy is called one of another race, a foreigner, for he was not a Jew" (1975:684). Another factor to keep in mind is the care that Luke takes to show that these converts of Samaria are unable to experience the full benefits of the messianic message through the ministry of Peter and John. If they are Jews then how is it that they need such care and attention from Jerusalem? Though of less importance in Luke's narrative, Jerusalem's interest in the Samaritans seems to parallel in some ways Peter's later ministry to Cornelius in chapters 10–11 (8:16; 11:1-3).

Although the Samaritans are not Jews, they are religiously very close to Judaism and therefore cannot be said to be Gentiles. Luke's point in recording the story of the Samaritans is to indicate that the gospel is embracing a group of people who have been historically excluded from Jewry, thus edging this young movement away from the fierce particularism that characterized Judaism. The relationship between Jews and Samaritans parallels at some points the relationship between blacks and whites in the United States. Preaching the gospel to Samaritans represents an obvious cultural step in the movement of the gospel. But apart from the word foreigner, noted above, the reader might think that the Samaritans were some kind of minority group within Jewry. They are definitely not Gentiles in Luke's understanding. Luke gives almost no information on the cultural differences between Jews and Samaritans. But when he narrates the care with which Jerusalem incorporates them into the Christian movement, which, for Luke, is a theological point, this indicates that a major cultural step has been taken in the gospel becoming universal. The church has taken a major step in overcoming historic racism.

The Ethiopian Eunuch

Luke's inclusion of the Ethiopian eunuch continues to be one of the most puzzling episodes found in Acts 6 to 15. There are some indications in the text that this man was a proselyte to Judaism. He has been to Jerusalem to worship and is reading a scroll of Isaiah when encountered by Philip. It seems also that Philip has no trouble explaining the gospel to him, indicating that his religious background had sufficiently prepared him to understand the message Philip would preach to Jews. But Luke's failure to call him a proselyte indicates that he was not a convert to Judaism (cp. Ac 6:5).

Gaventa's first inclination, in her study of this episode, is to call the eunuch a Gentile because his physical disability, according to Deuteronomy 23:1, would prevent him from becoming a proselyte (1986:104). After a thorough discussion of the three conversion stories found in Acts 8–11 Gaventa says: "...he is neither the first Gentile convert *nor* a proselyte to Judaism. Instead, he symbolizes all those from earth's end who, unlike Jerusalem Jews, will receive the gospel" (1986:123).

While Gaventa may be right, the physical condition of the man may give the best clue as to his place in Luke's narrative. As was mentioned above, the law of Moses forbade a blemished person from entering the congregation of the Lord (Dt 23:1). Could Luke also be making the point that this man represents one of those marginal characters (like the sinners and tax gatherers of Lk 15:1; and even the Samaritans) who, though completely unacceptable within Judaism, find ready acceptance within the messianic movement? This interpretation would certainly be consistent with the view that Luke is showing the gospel moving progressively from particularism to universalism. Luke not only introduces this man as an Ethiopian eunuch but persistently refers to this man as a eunuch (vv. 32, 34, 36 and 39). On every occasion when Luke refers to him in personal terms, including when he is introduced, he makes it known that the man was a eunuch. This may be an indication that for Luke, though this man tried to find answers to his need within Judaism, he was unable because of his handicap and the exclusion of the law. But when he hears the messianic message he experiences God's joy (v. 39). This eunuch from the borders of the world, having failed to find answers to his spiritual need in Jerusalem, finds understanding and acceptance from God through the gospel preached by Philip. Thus Luke shows the gospel crossing another threshold in the direction of the Gentiles. Luke's account alerts the reader to another cultural step being taken in the gospel becoming universal.

Conclusion

Three significant changes in the makeup of the Jewish messianic movement are introduced in Acts 6–8. The Hellenists are recognized and affirmed as Hellenists with their own leadership. Second, the Samaritans with their long history of bitter feelings and hatred between themselves and Jews are embraced by the Jerusalem church and included as full members of the church as Samaritans. The third change comes through the recognition and acceptance of a man previously disqualified to enter the Temple because of a physical handicap. Through these episodes radical changes in the fundamental makeup of the Jewish church are taking place.

Personal Response and Reflection

1.   What role do the Hellenists play in Luke's story of the gospel moving from the particular to the universal?

2.   From your study of this chapter along with Luke's account of Stephen, what would you say was Stephen's most significant contribution to early Christianity?

3.   What parallels do you see between the tensions of Hebrews and Hellenists and the tensions between groups in the church today?

4.   What parallels do you see between the Samaritans and Jews and different groups throughout the world today?

5

Cornelius:
The Paradigmatic Conversion

Questions to Consider before Reading this Chapter

*Suppose that a group of Sawi people from Irian Jaya visited your church on a Sunday morning. They want to see an authentic expression of Christianity. What would they see? How much of the service would be *biblical? Cultural?*

*What are some of the common obstacles you encounter when communicating the gospel? Name some theological and cultural barriers.

*Before reading the chapter, review Acts 9:32-11:18. What do you think is Luke's primary message in this section of his narrative?

There is no episode any more central in Luke's presentation of the story of Christianity than his account of the conversion of Cornelius. On the events of this section Luke places the full weight of his historical and theological argument for the universality of the gospel message (cf. 15:8-11, 13ff.). Because this account is quite lengthy, the first task in interpreting this episode will be to briefly summarize the story. This will be done by dividing Acts 9:32-11:18 into eight scenes following the approach used by Gaventa (1986:96-129). This summary will be followed by a brief analysis especially focusing on Cornelius and Peter. This chapter will conclude with an evaluation of the cross-cultural elements found in this story.

Summary of Acts 9:32–11:18

Scene One: 9:32-43: Luke sets the stage for Peter's encounter with Cornelius by beginning with two stories from Peter's itinerant ministry. He begins this episode with this statement: "*As* Peter traveled about the country . . . " (9:32). Luke's use of the word "as" gives the kind of vagueness about when this occurred that he wishes to convey. In this way Peter's ministry to Cornelius, unlike Saul's conversion and the founding of the church in Antioch, was not in any way associated with or influenced by Stephen's martyrdom nor the Hellenists.

Almost all discussions of Peter's ministry to Cornelius begin with chapter 10, but it seems that Luke wants his reader to be aware of what Peter was doing prior to introducing Cornelius. In 9:32-43 he briefly tells of two episodes that demonstrate Peter's continued ability to perform signs and wonders (Ac 5:14-16). The first story involves the healing of a paralytic named Aeneas in the town of Lydda. The second story is the raising of the woman Dorcas from the dead in the city of Joppa. Luke closes his introduction of this section with Peter in the house of Simon the Tanner in Joppa. These two cities, Lydda and Joppa, are about thirty and thirty-five miles, respectively, northwest of Jerusalem along the Mediterranean coast. Until Herod the Great built Caesarea, thirty miles north of Joppa, Joppa was the only natural port city along this coast (Douglas 1962:654).

Luke conveys the following important facts in this brief account. First, Peter is traveling outside of Jerusalem, thereby indicating that he is no longer involved in the day-by-day leadership in Jerusalem. This could also point to some type of leadership change going on in Jerusalem. And, incidentally, there may be some kind of hint here that the other apostles were also involved in ministry outside of Jerusalem. If so, this would agree with Luke's subsequent report that James and a group of elders were leading the church in Jerusalem (11:30; 12:17; 15:5ff.). Second, there are already Christians in these towns (9:36—"a disciple named Tabitha"). This is only the second time Luke has made the reader aware of the spread of Christianity outside of Jerusalem without giving any information as to how the gospel was taken to these cities (9:1-19). It is also important to note that Peter is ministering exclusively within a Jewish context. There seems to be no intent on his part to evangelize Gentiles. Chapter 10 emphatically confirms this. This is also consistent with Luke's overall record that the Gentile mission, while opened and supported by the apostles, was carried out exclusively by non-apostolic Christians.

Scene Two: 10:1-8 introduces the reader to Cornelius and tells of the vision that results in his sending three men from his home in Caesarea to Joppa to get Peter. Cornelius is said to be a Roman soldier from Italy. He is thus a Gentile, but the text indicates he is "devout and God-fearing" (10:2, 22). He is also said to be generous to the poor and prays at the stated Jewish prayer times. In short, this man, while not a proselyte, is in every sense of the word a pious person from the Jewish standpoint. This Gentile soldier would not be unlike the centurion found in Luke 7:1-10. This angelic vision instructs Cornelius to send for Peter.

Scene Three: 10:9-16—While the messengers are on their way to Joppa to get Peter and are nearing the city, Peter goes up on the rooftop at noontime to pray and await his meal.

Peter falls into a trance and has a vision of a sheet being let down out of heaven. In the sheet he sees four-footed beasts, reptiles and birds, three basic categories of animal life in Jewish culture. A voice which he recognizes as the Lord's commands him to kill and eat these creatures. Peter adamantly refuses to defile himself. Peter's refusal to eat these unclean animals should not be interpreted as disobedience on his part. Peter's refusal is based on his commitment to the Mosaic law and is an indication of his orthodoxy. This vision is repeated three times leaving Peter wondering as to its meaning.

Scene Four: 10:17-23a—While Peter is puzzling over the vision the three men sent by Cornelius from Caesarea arrive at Joppa. The Holy Spirit tells Peter: "Do not hesitate to go with them, for I have sent them" (v. 20). When Peter meets them at the gate they tell him of Cornelius' request. After hearing their story the text says, "Peter invited the men into the house to be his guests" (v. 23). While perhaps somewhat unusual, inviting Gentiles in a Jewish home would not require a Jew to compromise on the foods he ate.

Scene Five: 10: 23b-33—The next day, Peter, with six believing fellow Jews, travels with Cornelius' men back to Caesarea. Arriving at Cornelius' house, Peter finds it filled with Cornelius' friends and relatives. Peter tells Cornelius: "You are well aware that it is against our law for a Jew to associate with a Gentile or visit him. But God has shown me that I should not call any man impure or unclean" (v. 28). This serves as a commentary by Luke witnessing to the orthodox beliefs and practice of Peter. Peter remains mystified as to why Cornelius has sent for him (v. 29). Peter's response differs noticeably from his usual response at opportunities to preach the gospel. In Acts 2, 3, 4 and 5 Peter preaches the gospel in very diverse and difficult circumstances. Why is Peter so reluctant to preach the gospel to these people? Cornelius then tells Peter of his vision and concludes with an invitation for Peter to speak God's words to him and his friends (vv. 30-33).

Scene Six: 10:34-43—Peter's message, after a brief statement about his own "conversion," is similar to other messages given to *Jewish* audiences in Acts with the exception of a greater accent on the ministry of Jesus and less emphasis on the resurrection and exaltation (2:22ff.; 3:12ff.). The few things Luke includes in the ministry of Christ seem appropriate for a first-century Roman soldier. He says that "God anointed Jesus of Nazareth with the Holy Spirit and power, and . . . went around doing good and healing all who were under the power of the devil, because God was with him" (v. 38). Next Peter tells these Gentiles of the free nature of the gospel of Jesus.

Scene Seven: 10:44-48—As Peter tells of the forgiveness that can be found by faith in Jesus, these Gentiles suddenly begin speaking in tongues. The Holy Spirit "falls" on all of the Gentiles gathered in the room. The Jews who have accompanied Peter "were astonished that the gift of the Holy Spirit had been poured out even on the Gentiles." At Peter's urging, these Jews baptize Cornelius and his household. At the request of these new Gentile converts Peter and his Jewish friends remain a few days with Cornelius.

Scene Eight: 11:1-18—The news of the response of the Gentiles precedes Peter's arrival back in Jerusalem and on his arrival "those of the circumcision" confront Peter because he "went into the house of uncircumcised men and ate with them" (11:3). From verse 4 through verse 15 Luke recounts in abbreviated form all that has occurred in chapter 10. The only new information that comes out in this recap, and the reader has been kept in suspense about this, is that Peter's mission to Cornelius was evangelistic (v. 14). One noticeable difference in the order of the events is that Peter begins his explanation, not with the vision of Cornelius, but with his vision of the sheet let down out of heaven. While out of sequence, it has the advantage of addressing immediately their question about eating with Gentiles (v. 3). Peter holds his Jewish colleagues in suspense about the experience of Cornelius until he tells of his arrival at Cornelius' house. At this time Peter tells his interrogators that Cornelius had been commanded by an angel to send for him. Peter's ministry to Cornelius includes visions, trances, angels and the direct ministry of the Holy Spirit.

Peter's defense forces him to interpret this amazing event. Peter's interpretation of this event in verses 15-17 relates this episode to the promise of Christ—". . . you will be baptized with the Holy Spirit"—and with their own personal pentecostal experience. He concludes his defense by saying: "So if God gave them the same gift as he gave us, who believed in the Lord Jesus Christ, who was I to think that I could oppose God?" (v. 17). Peter's language here reminds the reader of the kind of language the apostles used when attacked by the Sanhedrin (4:19-20). Implied in Peter's question is the possibility that the Christian church, like the Sanhedrin, could find themselves in a position of rebelling against God. This would, of course, include Luke's readers. To refuse to recognize that God has included the Gentiles in the gospel is to find oneself in opposition to God himself. Peter's defense fully satisfies the church in Jerusalem and they exclaim, not, "now it is clear that Jews can eat with Gentiles," as their question in verse 3 would seem to call for, but, rather, "so then, God has granted even the Gentiles repentance unto life" (v. 18). Their premise seems to be that if Jews can eat with Gentiles, then Gentiles have become clean.

Analysis of Cornelius' Conversion

In her analysis of this story (10:1-11:18), Gaventa (1986:111-112) sees a constant pattern of some event in Cornelius' life followed by an event in Peter's, and this order repeated until the end of the story. She summarizes this literary pattern in this way:

Literary Pattern—Acts 10:1 -11:18		
Theme	Person(s)	Text
Vision Scene	1 Cornelius	10:1-8
	2 Peter	10:9-16
Journey& Welcome	3 Cornelius	10:17-23a
	4 Peter	10:23b-29
Proclamation	5 Cornelius	10:30-33
	6 Peter	10:34-43
Confirmation	7 Holy Spirit	10:44-48
	8 Community	11:1-18

Gaventa believes that Luke has deliberately placed the stories of the eunuch, Paul and Cornelius in sequence to show the fulfillment of Acts 1:8 (1986:123-125). The Ethiopian eunuch "symbolizes all those from earth's end who, unlike Jerusalem Jews, *will* receive the gospel" (1986:123). Paul symbolizes an enemy of the church whom God is able to overcome and bring into the Christian movement. Cornelius represents the firstfruits from the Gentiles.

There is little debate as to the major purpose of Acts 9:32–11:18 in Luke's overall narrative. As Gaventa says: "The conclusion to which Luke points is unmistakable: God has included the Gentiles, and the church may not resist. . . . Not only is the decision unmistakable, but it forms the climax of the first half of Acts, with 11:19–15:35 forming the denouement" (1986:122). Luke uses the story of Cornelius as a paradigmatic account of Gentile conversions and thereby demonstrates beyond any question that the traditional requirement for Gentiles to become a part of God's people— circumcision and the offering of sacrifices—has been decisively changed. God has granted to the Gentiles repentance *qua* Gentiles. Luke has done a masterful job of leading the reader step by step toward this moment, beginning with the birth of Jesus all the way through the conversion of Saul, so that what emerges is a universal faith, for Jews and Gentiles alike. In this regard Luke has shown himself to be an artistic writer par excellence. Luke's threefold repetition of Cornelius' conversion is a part of his literary style in demonstrating its theological importance (10:1-48; 11:1-18; 15:8-11, 13). Luke has accomplished his task of showing God as the dominant *actor* throughout this episode, (and throughout Luke-Acts), not humans. It is God who sovereignly brings Cornelius and Peter together.

Reflections on Cornelius' Conversion

It might be assumed that when Luke comes to this account of the conversion of a Gentile he would be vitally interested in the cultural implications of this process. And he is. But perhaps not in the way one would expect. Who is this story really about? Is it only about Cornelius? While the story revolves around both Cornelius and Peter, Luke follows it back into the Jewish context and never returns to give any clues as to how this new Gentile fellowship assimilated these events into their own experience and worked out some of the obvious pastoral problems that would arise out of their experience with Christ. Luke is interested in the reader arriving at the same conclusion as the Jews in Jerusalem (11:18).

Cornelius' Status

Does Luke want his reader to see Cornelius as a Gentile? As inappropriate as this question may seem, a close examination of the text indicates how pertinent it really is. What cultural and theological changes does this man have to make in order to become a Christian? Luke has painted this man with such pious strokes that he almost appears to be a proselyte to Judaism before Peter meets him. While his religious practices make him very close to the Jewish faith, he is not a proselyte but a God-fearer (10:2, 22; 11:3). The fundamental difference between a God-fearer and a proselyte would be in such matters as circumcision and the observance of the Jewish food laws (Segal 1988:336-369). Whereas Jews might have been impressed with such Gentiles, religiously they were just like other Gentiles when it came to table fellowship (11:3). But from the standpoint of the direction of the messianic movement and the message it is preaching, the synagogue-attending God-fearer would be very much like the Jew. When Paul preaches to a synagogue audience, which includes Jews and Gentiles, he gives his message a messianic cast (13:16; 17:2, 3). Looked at this way the Gentile God-fearer would have to make little more cultural change than a Jew in order to become a Christian. Of course Luke makes little effort to point out the cultural changes necessary in order for Cornelius to be saved. In fact the narrative makes clear that it would be much easier from a cultural standpoint for Cornelius and his household to convert to Christianity than it would for them to become proselytes to Judaism. But the same cannot be said for Peter and the Jews. According to Luke the theological implications of Gentiles becoming Christians is much greater for the Jews than the Gentile God-fearers.

The "Conversion" of Peter

What happened to Peter here in chapter 10 (and thus to the messianic movement) was perhaps more important, and certainly much more demanding psychologically and intellectually, than what happened to Cornelius. From one standpoint the conversion of the Gentiles was no problem for God; the difficulty was in bringing the Jewish Christians to see that Gentiles did not need to become Jews as they became Christians. What are the cultural implications for Jewish Christians of the first century if Gentiles become Christians without the traditional requirements of circumcision and kosher eating? One of the matters that surfaces in this chapter is that of table-fellowship. The nature of Christianity as outlined in the early chapters of Acts demonstrates the intimate relationship that developed in the charismatic community. They experienced the life of Christ in the most intimate of ways, sharing their faith along with food, possessions, and even their houses. The level of intimacy would be completely unfathomable to these Jewish Christians with their long history of religious practices that distinguished them and enabled them to maintain ritual purity.

Biblical/Missiological Lessons

The mission to the Gentiles has been decided. There can be no turning back. The process of working out this giant step in the mission to the Gentiles will take some years yet, but with Peter's mission to Cornelius God's will has become clear. Peter makes this point later in the Jerusalem council (15:7-11). Here are some of the biblical/missiological lessons that can be drawn from this episode.

God's Will and Work Take Place Within the Particular

Prior to this episode both Peter and Cornelius were certain that God revealed himself only within the Jewish people and faith. This belief was based on how God had worked since the time of Abraham. Even after the Great Commission had been given and all that had occurred in the messianic movement, Peter and his fellow-Jews (11:1-18) were convinced that Jewish faith and culture were the only vehicles capable of expressing the will and purpose of God.

From a cultural standpoint Jews could not distinguish between their culture and the gospel. They were both the same to them. Therefore, to know God was to become a Jew, i.e., to adopt Jewish culture. This explains why the apostles did not rush out and evangelize Gentiles after the Great Commission. Their slowness in evangelizing Gentiles cannot be attributed to disobedience, nor spiritual dullness, but rather to the need of understanding the distinction between their historic faith and the gospel. This could only be discovered through a process involving struggle, doubt, experience and God's gracious intervention.

The Gospel is Liberated from Particularism and Becomes a Universal Message

From this story of Peter's mission to Cornelius the following observations can be made. The message of God can no longer be limited to any one cultural expression of faith. God willed that his revelation be conveyed to the world through a particular people/culture. Now it has become clear that the gospel can be preached to any people without calling on them to abandon their culture.

Second, following this line of reasoning it can be said that God's message is *supracultural*. Although God's message comes to us in human language and symbols, ultimately the message cannot be contained in human culture. God's message is above or outside of culture. But for God's message to be understood it must be communicated in cultural terms. The gospel expressed in the Korean language and culture cannot be understood by the Masai of Kenya, Africa. The Masai must hear the gospel in their own language and cultural forms.

Therefore the task of the early church and the church today is the contextualization of the message from generation to generation and from culture to culture. To put it rather crudely, the gospel in its pure form is naked and the task of missions is to clothe it appropriately. For the Westerner these clothes may be a double-breasted suit and for the Motilone of South America these clothes may be a G-string.

When Don and Carol Richardson went to work among the Sawi people in Irian Jaya, Indonesia, they learned the Sawi language and began preaching the gospel to them as they would have to people in North America, with some minor adaptations. This gospel was boring and incomprehensible to the Sawi people. It was only when Don and Carol learned about the peace child concept in the Sawi culture that they were able to put Sawi clothes on the gospel. The peace child analogy arising out of Sawi history and culture proved to be one of the means of contextualizing the gospel for this people (Richardson 1974).

Conclusion

Why does God have to move heaven and earth to get Peter to go to Cornelius? With all of Peter's background of spending three years with Jesus, hearing the Great Commission, experiencing Pentecost, accepting Hellenists and Samaritans, God still cannot get him to the Gentiles without visions, trances, angels and the Holy Spirit! And even after he arrives at the house of Cornelius he is still uncertain about what his task is—"may I ask why you sent for me?" (10:29). Luke shows in an emphatic way that Peter is an orthodox Jew who has no idea that Gentiles should be evangelized as Gentiles. The mission to the Gentiles occurs as a process that is only gradually realized over a number of years and through a series of events and discussions.

In this way Luke shows that the theological challenge of the Gentile mission is not the reluctance of the Gentiles to respond to the gospel but the traditional Jewish belief that Gentiles must also accept the cultural forms of Jewishness. While Luke's account of Cornelius' conversion clearly establishes his point that Gentiles can now become Christians, his account of Peter's struggle demonstrates that the "conversion" of the Jewish Christians must precede Gentile conversions. Jewish Christians must drop historic standards that excluded Gentiles. Peter must go to the home of Cornelius and remain there after Cornelius' conversion; Cornelius does not come to Peter. Whether the difficulties involved in preaching the gospel cross-culturally are sociological or theological, these objections must be overcome. The gospel must be preached to those who have never heard. Luke's narrative demonstrates that the "conversion" of the messenger must precede the conversion of those who are lost.

Luke's narrative of the conversion of a Gentile household becomes paradigmatic for early Christianity and becomes a biblical standard for all subsequent cross-cultural mission. The gospel that has been bound up with the particular is liberated. Subsequently, every people group that embraces the gospel has an obligation to preach this gospel to other people groups without requiring them to change their culture. This missionary urgency continues throughout church history.

Personal Response and Reflection

1. Why did the Messianic Jews in Jerusalem "take issue" with Peter when he returned from his time with Cornelius (Ac 11:2)? What were the key issues for them? Can you think of issues that parallel this in churches today?

2. Is human culture an obstacle to overcome or an asset to be employed when it comes to communicating the gospel cross-culturally? Explain.

3. Dollar writes: *Therefore the task of the early church and the church today is the contextualization of the message from generation to generation and from culture to culture. To put it rather crudely, the gospel in its pure form is naked and the task of mission is to put the appropriate clothes on the gospel* (p. 87). What does it mean to "clothe the gospel"? What are some practical skills a missionary must have to be appropriately equipped to contextualize the good news?

6

The Jerusalem Council:
Nailing it Down

Questions to Consider before
Reading this Chapter

*How are pastoral, theological and missiological problems solved by the church today? One large issue facing the church today: should women be ordained as pastors? How do you think the evangelical church should resolve this issue? Read Acts 15:1-35 to see how the early church resolved the question of whether Gentiles needed to be circumcised.

*What adjustments in worship style have to be made when people from different cultural backgrounds meet together? Musical adjustments? Preaching adjustments?

The Jerusalem Council stands at the center of Luke's narrative of early Christianity. All of Luke's narrative has been leading to this moment. All that happens after this chapter is meant to expand, clarify and draw out the implications of what was decided at this council. Marshall says: "Luke's account of the discussion regarding the relation of the Gentiles to the law of Moses forms the centre of Acts both structurally and theologically" (1980:242). The background of this section is Peter's mission to Cornelius and the impact made by Paul and Barnabas' mission launched from Antioch. A brief comment on Acts 13 and 14 will provide enough information needed to discuss Acts 15.

Paul and Barnabas' Mission in Acts 13–14

There were multiple leaders in the Antiochene church (13:1). Luke lists five leaders of the church. Two of them, Simeon and Lucius, seem to have been Hellenists; Manaen had a "royal" background; and the last two, Barnabas and Paul, were comfortable and skilled in both the Hebrew context and the diaspora context. Although raised in the diaspora, they also had very close ties with Jerusalem and Pharisaic Judaism.

Luke grounds his brief account of the launching of the mission from Antioch in pneumatology (13:2, 4). The Holy Spirit, having launched this vanguard effort, is also the one who gives Barnabas and Saul their first breakthrough in Gentile ministry (13:9ff). This breakthrough takes place in the province of Cyprus, in the court of the proconsul, Sergius Paulus, in Paphos. Barnabas has been leading the team, but when both of them were threatened by a "magician," Saul is thrust forward by the Holy Spirit. "Saul," now Paul, confronts this opponent of the gospel, Elymas (Bar Jesus), convinces the proconsul of the truth, and then assumes decisive leadership of the team (13:13). Having taken charge of the mission, Paul takes a radical direction by breaking into the hinterlands of Pamphylia (rather than traveling the natural route east or west along the northern coast of the Mediterranean) until they reach the Roman city of Antioch near Pisidia in the southwestern corner of Galatia. Following their established custom (13:5) Paul makes his way to the synagogue where Luke records Paul's first synagogue sermon. The response to this sermon and the exchange between Paul and the Jews is decisive for Paul's entire ministry (13:13-31).

Within a week after this sermon Paul and Barnabas are forced out of the synagogue, having made their decision to preach to Gentiles (vv. 43-47). They continue ministering in the city until they are forced out by the Jew-Gentile opposition (48ff.). They follow the Roman road eastward to Iconium where a similar pattern of initial reception in the synagogue followed by rejection, first by Jews, then by Gentiles, repeats itself. Paul preaches to a "pagan" audience in Lystra where he is, in turn, worshipped and later stoned (14:10-20). After making "many disciples" at Derbe, Paul and Barnabas return to each of the cities where they had preached. After encouraging these disciples and establishing leadership, they finally return to Antioch, Syria, where they report in detail of how God had "opened the door of faith to the Gentiles" (14:22ff., 27).

In Luke's schematization of early Christianity, Acts 13–14 function to drive home the conclusions reached in Peter's mission to Cornelius. Here the reader learns how the gospel extends to Gentiles in the broader Greco-Roman world and extends further and further from Jerusalem. While the churches established on this journey are made up of a mixture of Jews and Gentiles, the emphasis in the report of this mission is on the Gentile response. It also becomes apparent that the gospel is impacting people who have had little or no contact with the Jewish faith. Paul and Barnabas' mission in Asia Minor is the final experiential step in the gospel becoming universal before the church council in Jerusalem.

Large numbers of Gentiles becoming Christians increases the apprehension of some of the Jewish Christians. It takes some years for this opposition to develop and become organized. Antioch is the center of the Gentile church and the Gentile mission. Thus when Luke says, "Some men came down from Judea to Antioch and were teaching the brothers: 'Unless you are circumcised according to the custom taught by Moses, you cannot be saved,'" it becomes clear that a major formal decision on the legitimacy of the Gentile mission must be made.

There will be two issues explored in this chapter. The first issue, and by far the more important, is the question of how Luke understands the relationship of the Gentiles to circumcision and the whole Mosaic system. The second question revolves around the decree that holds such a prominent place in the decision of the Jerusalem Council concerning the obligation it placed on Gentile believers. This decree will be discussed as it relates to the question of the Mosaic law. The relationship of the decree to the question of table-fellowship between Jews and Gentiles will be discussed in chapter 9.

The Decision Regarding Circumcision

Luke opens chapter 15 with a brief paragraph that sets forth the basic issue confronting the Jerusalem Council. The discussion as to whether Gentiles had to be circumcised originated in Antioch during the time that Paul and Barnabas were present following their first missionary trip. Regarding this Luke reports that "some men . . . from Judea" came down to Antioch "teaching the brethren, 'unless you are circumcised according to the custom of Moses, you cannot be saved'" (15:1).

Paul and Barnabas adamantly oppose any imposition of Jewish rites on Gentile converts. The very "sharp dispute and debate" that follows fails to resolve the issue (v. 2). When the question could not be settled locally, Paul and Barnabas, along with others, are sent by the church in Antioch to Jerusalem to resolve the issue once for all. A note of celebration permeates the narrative of the Antiochene delegation's journey to Jerusalem. They are passing through Phoenicia and Samaria reporting to the churches the response of the Gentiles to the gospel. This "made all the brothers very glad" (v. 3). Arriving in Jerusalem these delegates from Antioch are welcomed by the church, but "believers who belonged to the party of the Pharisees stood up and said, 'The Gentiles must be circumcised and required to obey the law of Moses'" (vv. 4-5).

The fundamental issue that occasions this conference revolves around whether Gentile Christians have to follow the traditional requirement of circumcision. Luke implies that this issue had already been settled by the majority of the churches in Antioch, Phoenicia, Samaria and probably even in Jerusalem itself because only the converts from the Pharisees in Jerusalem insist on Gentile circumcision (v. 5). There is, then, according to Luke, only a small, tenacious minority within the Jewish Christian community that insists on circumcising Gentiles. This is in contrast to chapter 11:1-3 where resistance characterizes all of the Jerusalem church, including the apostles themselves. There is no indication that any of the leadership in the church of Jerusalem or Antioch opposed the inclusion of Gentiles. But the very fact that it requires such a high level discussion points to the need of a clear and final decision on the part of the whole church. The question of circumcision is not to be seen as an isolated aspect of Judaism, but rather a shorthand way of referring to the entire Mosaic system (v. 5).

Peter's Argument

After much debate (v. 7) Peter speaks to the council (vv. 8-11). His entire presentation comes from his experience with Cornelius along with theological reflections on the implications of what happened there. Luke makes the following things clear in his account of Peter's speech: First, Peter was chosen by God to open the door of faith to the Gentiles. For Luke's church it was important to verify that the initiative for Gentile evangelism, while coming from God himself, was taken by the apostles whom Jesus had chosen.

Secondly, the idea of Gentile evangelism and baptism did not originate with Peter or the apostles but ultimately belonged to God himself. God chose Peter to preach to these

Gentiles. Furthermore, when the Holy Spirit's sovereign actions bypassed any purpose or intent on Peter's part, falling on Cornelius and his household while Peter was still preaching, it thereby removes the Gentile mission from the realm of human initiative (10:44-48; 11:15a; 15:8). Thirdly, it was the work of the Holy Spirit in their life, apart from any rituals (implied), which was responsible for making the Gentiles *clean* . Lastly, and most surprising of all, Peter says: " . . . *we* (note the "we and they," and the "us and them" throughout Peter's speech) are saved in the same way as *they* are" (v. 11). Peter moves beyond the primary question of the conference and concludes that circumcision not only has nothing to do with the salvation of Gentiles, but it also has nothing to do with the salvation of the Jews.

Barnabas and Paul Testify

Barnabas and Paul, according to Luke, only give a testimony at this meeting. They tell of "signs and wonders" God had done among the Gentiles during their ministry (v. 12). Actually, in Luke's theology, signs and wonders play a crucial role in authenticating and enhancing the growth of the Christian movement (2:19, 22, 43; 4:30; 5:12; 6:8; 14:3; 15:12; see also 4:16, 22; 8:6, 13). The manifestation of signs and wonders demonstrates God's approval of the mission to the Gentiles.

James' Conclusion

The entire discussion is summarized and brought to a conclusion by James. He confirms what Peter has said and shows that this was God's purpose according to Scripture (15:13ff.). Luke assumes his readers will understand how this passage validates the decision not to circumcise Gentiles. It was obvious to these Jewish Christians of the first century that the "tabernacle of David" had been restored and thus the prerequisite for the reception of the Gentiles had been met. Bruce says the tabernacle of David being restored refers to the resurrection and exaltation of Jesus which must precede the mission to the Gentiles (1954:310). James argues that the salvation of the Gentiles is not a new idea thought up by Peter or any other human being but is part of God's predetermined plan.

It is possible to argue that God's promise to include the Gentiles (found in Amos) does not necessarily abrogate the requirement of circumcision. And this, of course, would be the normal understanding of this passage prior to what had happened in the decade preceding this Jerusalem council. But in the context of all that the church has experienced Luke can include a quote from an eschatological passage in Amos without explanation thereby proving that Gentiles need not be circumcised. This interpretation becomes apparent when James goes on to say that the Gentiles *should not be troubled* (v. 20).

For Luke this statement by James wraps up the whole issue and represents the unanimous consensus of the church made up of representatives from Jerusalem and Antioch. But James' final statement that "[Gentiles should] abstain from food polluted by idols, from sexual immorality, from the meat of strangled animals and from blood" has proven difficult to reconcile with the unambiguous decision that Gentiles do not have to be circumcised. This decree which contains the four prohibitions imposed by this council on the Gentile Christians will now be explored.

The Decree

The four prohibitions imposed on the Gentiles have provoked a great deal of discussion and debate, especially as these prohibitions are so closely related to the decision that Gentiles do not have to be circumcised in order to be saved. These prohibitions are repeated three times in the book of Acts (15:20, 29; 21:25) and are found nowhere else in the New Testament, not even in Galatians, Romans or 1 Corinthians. What is the relationship of this decree to the decision just made and to the Mosaic law? Do these prohibitions represent Luke's understanding that the Gentiles have at least a minimal obligation to the Mosaic law?

Definition of the Decree

The first command to "abstain from the pollutions of idols" refers to the eating of meat that has been offered to a pagan deity and then sold in the marketplace, or participating in a cultic ritual where such food was served (Marshall 1980:263; Haenchen 1971:449). The second command has to do with chastity. To modern readers this call for sexual purity may seem out of place in this list, but an awareness of the low sexual standards in Greco-Roman culture makes it quite comprehensible that Jews could be quickly offended by what might be considered the average practice of new Gentile Christians (Bruce 1951:300). Such sexual practices would make it difficult for Jews to eat with Gentiles because table-fellowship indicated approval of those at the table. The third prohibition has to do with "what is strangled" and refers to the Jewish requirement that animal meat be properly drained of blood before it is eaten (Haenchen 1971:449). The fourth and last command is very similar to the third one. Seifrid (1987:48) says that this command has to do with the prohibition against the eating of blood, as the Jews considered the life of the animal to be in the blood.

Verse 21 which follows the decree says: "For from early generations Moses has had in every city those who preach him, for he is read every Sabbath in the synagogues." Dibelius says: "Although straightforward from the linguistic and textual points of view, in context and meaning it is one of the most difficult verses in the New Testament" (1956:97). One of the obvious difficulties in this verse is to determine the exact meaning of the little connective "for." This connective seems to be giving a reason why the decree is necessary. Bruce (1988:295) argues that this decree is aimed at the relationship between Jewish Christians and Gentile Christians:

James therefore gave it as his considered judgment that Gentile Christians should be directed to avoid food which had idolatrous associations and the flesh of animals from which the blood had not been completely drained, and that they should conform to the Jewish code of relations between the sexes instead of remaining content with the pagan standards to which they had been accustomed.

And with this interpretation there seems to be a general agreement (Marshall 1980:254).

The Decree and the Mosaic Law

These prohibitions as recorded by Luke have the closest possible relationship to the decision that Gentiles do not have to be circumcised to be saved. It also seems clear from the setting Luke gives to this council in verses 1-5 that circumcision was an issue that symbolically represented the entire Mosaic law. There is a tension, then, between this decree, which appears to impose some obligation to the Jewish law on Gentiles, and the decision of the council that Gentiles are not obligated to the Mosaic law. Should this decree be seen as an understanding on Luke's part that the Gentiles have some obligation to the Mosaic law?

Luke's account does not give the source of these prohibitions. He does not use the usual "the scripture says," or, "the prophets have spoken" (1:20; 2:16, 25, 34; 4:25; 7:42, 49; 11:16; 13:32, 40, 47). Many scholars assume that Leviticus 17–18, which governs the life of aliens and strangers living in Palestine, is the background of these prohibitions (Haenchen 1971:448ff.; Marshall 1980:253). J. C. O'Neill says: ". . . the analogy of the observances laid down for the 'stranger within the gate' in Leviticus 17 and 18 is invoked to provide the four cultic requirements of the Decree" (1961:101).

But this widely accepted interpretation of the decree has not gone unchallenged. Seifrid, in his discussion of "Jesus and the Law in Acts," vehemently disagrees with this interpretation (1987:39-57). He says that "it is unlikely that the

Decree is directly connected to Leviticus 17-18, [or] the Noachian commandments, . . . " (1987:49). He argues that the term proselyte used to translate the word stranger in Leviticus 17–18 had undergone a radical change and by the first century a proselyte was in essence a Jew. His second argument is that there is no evidence that Judaism invoked Leviticus 17–18 for proselytes or God-fearers. Seifrid's third argument is that if this is the only responsibility of Gentiles to the law, then what about issues such as adultery and murder?

If the more commonly accepted interpretation is followed, that this decree is taken from Leviticus 17–18, then the conclusion that Gentiles do have some relationship to the law, however tenuous it may be, cannot be avoided. But if these prohibitions cannot be found to come out of the Mosaic law, according to Seifrid, then what is the source of their authority in this context? The whole question of Luke's theological understanding of the Mosaic law, providing a broader context for understanding this decree, needs to be considered briefly.

Gentiles Have Some Obligation to Mosaic Law

A number of studies have come out in recent years contending that although Acts may seem to give the impression that Gentiles have no obligation to the Mosaic law, closer inspection proves this view to be false (O'Neill 1961:99-116; Juel 1983:103ff.; Jervell 1972 and 1984:30ff.). O'Neill says that while Luke makes it clear that the requirement of Gentiles to be circumcised is out of the question, at the same time he teaches that "Gentiles are bound to observe the *relevant parts* of the Mosaic Law" (1961:101, 103, italics added). O'Neill's argues that the "relevant parts" have to do with guidelines for table-fellowship between Jews and Gentiles.

Jervell agrees with O'Neill that Gentiles have an obligation to the law. He says that the initial response of the Jews, when Gentiles started becoming Christians, was to accept the Gentiles without imposing any prohibitions, but as the influx of Gentiles increased over the years a certain apprehension began to creep into the Jewish church. Jervell says: "We have no indication that Jewish Christians demanded from Stephen, Antioch, Barnabas or Paul a law-obedient Gentile mission" (1984:32). Gradually, according to Jervell, this attitude changed and "Acts 15 and Galatians 2 lead to the conclusion that the church of Jerusalem in connection with the Council introduced a more conservative policy" (1972:32-33). This conservatism originated out of the conviction of Jewish Christians that Christianity was tied up with national Israel (1972:33).

Juel seems to be in basic agreement with Jervell. He says that Luke is careful all through his writings to show that all those associated with this movement were obedient to the law. For instance Luke shows Christ's parents as good law-abiding parents and even Jesus himself was careful to observe the law (Lk 1–3). This same pattern can be seen in Acts and the prohibitions given at this council should be no surprise to anyone who has followed Luke's narrative (Juel 1983:106ff.). Juel shows that there is one people of God and that the Gentiles are simply added to this family: "Gentiles had been included in the family, but there still existed for Luke only one Israel, one people of God faithful to the law, one history of salvation begun with the call of Abraham. For him, Israel's law was the sign of continuity" (1983:109).

Richard, in his analysis of the structure of Acts 15, comes to a similar conclusion. He says that there were two major decisions reached by the council. The first was that of "non-interference with the divine plan; Gentiles are turning to God and he is forming a new people. In effect, verse 19, along with verses 10, 24 and 28 constitutes a formal rejection of the Judaizing demand that Gentiles become proselytes" (1984:196). The second decision is a requirement for the Gentiles to avoid giving offense to Jewish believers. Gentiles will have to keep the laws regulating the status of resident aliens in the land of Israel outlined in Leviticus 17–18. This requirement "reveals a deeper and more radical understanding of Moses than that displayed by the believing Pharisees"

(1984:196). His conclusion is that Luke teaches that "the law of Moses continues to be valid for Jews as Jews and for Gentiles as Gentiles" (1984:197).

The Gentiles Have No Obligation to Mosaic Law

There are a number of difficulties raised by the arguments above. The first is the question of whether the decision about circumcision includes the entire Mosaic law. If it does, and this seems to be the reasoning, then how can the council come back and impose prohibitions that derive from the Mosaic law? The decision that Gentiles do not have to be circumcised means that they are not obligated to keep the Mosaic law. If the Mosaic law has lost its authority, then where does the authority for these prohibitions come from? There is also the question as to whether these prohibitions are relative from a historical and contextual standpoint. Were these guidelines only pertinent for Gentiles who were in contact with Jews who were regularly hearing the Mosaic law read in the synagogues every Sabbath? If they are relative in terms of history and context then they can no longer be placed in the category of *laws* for the Gentiles.

Seifrid's argument, mentioned earlier, that these prohibitions did not originate out of the Mosaic law seems rather persuasive in light of these problems. But one of the difficulties with his position also involves the question of authority. How can the council say that it is necessary for the Gentiles to obey these prohibitions if they do not come from the Mosaic law? Seifrid recognizes this problem and answers this objection by saying that Luke develops a whole new approach for the Christian on questions of ethics and morality. He says: "It becomes apparent that for Luke another ethic, one based on the messianic status of Jesus, has replaced the Mosaic law as the imperative which is incumbent on both the believing community and the world at large" (1987:40). He argues that if these prohibitions are rooted in the Mosaic law this would conflict with the decision just made by the council that salvation in Christ is law-free (1987:50). The authority for this decree finds its authority in Luke's understanding of the messianic reign. When the council says the Holy Spirit (15:28) guided them to this decision, they are thereby removing it from the realm of law and placing the question of ethical guidelines on a new base, on the authority of the messianic status of Jesus (1987:50-51).

Seifrid's arguments must be answered by those who see the decree as an indication of Luke's imposition of the *relevant parts* of the law on Gentiles. But at the same time his view has some of the same weaknesses as does the previous view. Neither of these views discusses the question of whether the decree was relative. Are these prohibitions universal in nature? Whether these prohibitions are rooted in the Mosaic law or in the messianic reign of Jesus, the question as to their universality and permanence remains. Both views seem to suggest that the prohibitions are permanent and binding for all time. Does not the fact that the council addressed these prohibitions to specific historical churches and not to others automatically place some kind of limitation on the decree (15:23b)? This argument will be pursued and pushed further in the chapter on table-fellowship in chapter 9.

Summary

In spite of the questions raised from an introduction of these prohibitions, there are a number of objectives accomplished by Luke in placing this chapter where he does in his narrative of the growing Christian movement.

The Centrality of Acts 15 in Lukan Theology

Acts 15 obviously contains very important clues to Luke's understanding of the Christian movement. A close reading of Luke's narrative shows that he can paint the most beautiful picture of the harmony and unity of the church in one scene and in the very next scene reveal that the church is passing through a serious crisis (cp. 4:32-37 with 5:1-11 and 5:12-42 with 6:1-6). In this regard it should be noted that Luke simply avoids any mention of the problem regarding circumcision at Antioch and during Barnabas' and Paul's ministry in Antioch and Asia Minor. He omits this issue until he can show in some detail how the church eventually dealt with the problem. For this reason Acts 15 gives significant clues to Luke's understanding of the relationship of Gentiles to the Mosaic law and of the relationship of believing Jews and Gentiles. There is also no evidence from Luke's record that any of the apostles or any of the other leaders in Jerusalem had questioned the decision reached by the church in Acts 11:18. Secondly, the earliest date for Gentile evangelism in Luke's record is found in Acts 10–11, which was probably around AD 40. This would only leave nine years between Cornelius' conversion and Acts 15.

Gentiles Do Not Have to Be Circumcised

This is the historic and revolutionary theological decision that is reached by the council, thereby ensuring that Christianity would not be a small sect relegated to the backwaters of culture and world history. Lukan scholars seldom reach any consensus on the teaching found in Acts, but on this matter they agree emphatically: Luke teaches unequivocally that Gentiles can become Christians without any obligation to the traditional rite of circumcision. This consensus can be traced to Luke's masterful literary skill, in not only stating this view so clearly in chapter 15, but in the very careful and schematic arrangement he has used in narrating the story of the Christian movement from its beginnings until this climactic moment.

Gentile Concessions Are Necessary

Many scholars would prefer to state that Luke's placing of the decree in such close proximity to the major decision about circumcision signals a theological perspective that Gentiles have at least some minimal obligation to the Jewish law based on Leviticus 17–18. Others would reject this understanding by saying that Luke roots these ethical guidelines in the authority of Christ rather than the law. Neither view answers the question as to their permanency and universality. For Luke there is no tension between the abrogation of circumcision and obedience to the law and the imposition of this decree. Whatever view is taken as to the origin or purpose of the decree, it is certain that Gentile Christians are asked to accommodate the scruples of Jewish Christians.

The Unity of the Church

Luke is concerned with maintaining and promoting the unity of the church in his story. As disagreements arise in this growing movement Luke shows them being resolved (6:1ff.; 8:16ff.; 15:1ff.; for a possible exception cp. 15:36ff. But this is a personal conflict). A stress on unity is especially true in chapter 15 when he shows how the early church handled its most difficult problem. Through the process of intense and open dialogue the Jerusalem council gradually came to a unanimous decision. Luke leaves the impression that this decision was completely supported by all parts of the church, never to be raised again. All the participants, including missionaries like Paul and Barnabas and Christian Pharisees, came to a full agreement on this far-reaching issue. Luke leaves the reader marveling at the unity of the church as the council resolves this momentous question (15:30-35).

There Is One Church Made Up of Jews and Gentiles

This conference is an historic one, not only from a theological standpoint, but also from a psychological standpoint. The church has taken a quantum leap in understanding her self-identity. While in the past Gentiles could become a part of God's people only by losing their own cultural identity, now they can hold to their cultural identity with only minor alterations. Further, Gentiles do not form their own fellowship groups when they become Christians but are brought into a relationship with another group, the Jewish believers, who are also allowed to maintain their own cultural identity, with only minor alterations. The Christian movement is made up of both Jews and Gentiles. God has acted in a sovereign and unprecedented way in bringing Gentiles into a faith relationship with Jesus and with the Jewish people.

Reflections on the Jerusalem Council

The decision to allow Gentiles to bypass the historic requirement of circumcision marks the theological high point of Acts. It also represents a cultural high point of Acts. That this decision is replete with implications for missiology is obvious. When Jews, who for 2,000 years have remained separate from Gentiles, now accept them as members of the same spiritual family, this represents a revolutionary adaptation. But, as in all of his narrative, Luke views this process in theological categories which limits the number of sociological details. He is concerned with promoting the universality of the gospel and the oneness of the people of God.

Gentiles Do Not Have to Be Circumcised

While recording the momentous decision that Gentiles do not have to be circumcised, Luke narrates the decision in such a careful way that the reader, while realizing that decision has been made, is led into it almost imperceptibly; quite unlike the way Paul states it in Galatians 1–2. Even in Acts 15 Luke never comes out and says emphatically, "Gentiles *do not* have to be circumcised." On both occasions when the decision is announced Luke uses language that leaves no doubt about what has been decided and at the same time appears as non-threatening as possible to those Jews who might find the decision offensive. The first announcement is stated in this way: "Therefore my judgment is that *we should not trouble those of the Gentiles* who turn to God . . . " (15:19). The second says: "it has seemed good to the Holy Spirit and to us *to lay upon you no greater burden than these things . . . "* (15:28). While the overall impression created by Luke's narrative, including the two statements above, leaves no doubt as to what decision has been made, Luke's style enables his readers to adjust their minds to the full implications of the decision. By avoiding the cultural implications of this decision, e.g., circumcision has lost its theological content, but at the same time implying it, Luke perhaps makes it a little more palatable to those having the strongest negative reaction to this decision.

Gentiles Have to Observe Some Guidelines

The prohibitions imposed on Gentiles are stated in much stronger language and much more emphatically than the decision regarding circumcision. This decree is repeated three times by Luke, twice in Acts 15 and once in Acts 21. Luke repeats only a few items three times in Acts, such as Stephen's death, Paul's conversion, Cornelius' conversion and the rejection of the Jews. What is Luke's intention in recording this prohibition three times? This may be another way Luke has of taking the sting (for Jews) out of the decision to do away with the requirement of circumcision for Gentiles. Although the decision to impose the decree on Gentile Christians has cultural implications, Luke does not pursue this. Gentile Christians will have to embrace new guidelines on eating and sexual conduct, thus changing their lifestyle at specific points. Are these prohibitions given to govern and make possible table-fellowship between Jews and Gentiles? This is the central issue discussed in chapter 9.

Personal Response and Reflection

1.   Do you consider the arguments of Peter, Barnabas and Paul, and James to be biblical? That is, do they argue their points from the Old Testament Scriptures, or from their own experience? Explain your answer.

2. From your understanding of Acts and using any sources you want to, why does Luke give Barnabas and Paul only one verse (v. 12) in his account of the Jerusalem council? Also comment on the order of their names, i.e, *Barnabas and Paul!*

3. Name two issues facing the church today that are of major significance. What personal issue do you face right now that you find difficult in deciding whether it is biblical? Does the decision-making process of the early church give you any assistance in your own issue? How?

PART 3

Missiological Application

The missiological implications of Luke's story have been included throughout this study. But these last three chapters differ somewhat in seeking to apply Luke's insights to specific issues in the mission of the church today. There will of necessity be some repetition in these chapters. But this repetition will be along the lines of some of the more fundamental issues found in Luke-Acts bearing on the world mission of the church. Luke's story of the gospel moving from the particular to the universal has a great deal to say to the church today in its responsibility of reaching the unreached. It is in the area of application that the church has found the most difficulty in applying Luke's message.

This exhortation for the church today to be like the church in Acts, while not wholly inappropriate, often misses the point of Acts. The book of Acts contains a challenge for the church today mainly in its commitment and experience in missions. Luke does not have a great deal to say about the day-to-day pastoral life of the church. Rather, his challenge speaks more to the issues of process and relationships as they have to do with the church's universal nature and mission.

Chapter 7 in this section will be a discussion of the place of the apostolic Twelve in the mission to the Gentiles. This chapter will review some of the issues raised in Part Two, with a special focus on Peter and the Twelve as they grew in their understanding of universalism. It also touches on the question of Luke's purpose in writing the book of Acts. More specifically, this chapter will argue that the apostles do serve as helpful models for the church today as it engages in frontier missions. Chapter 8 continues this discussion of frontier missions by looking at Luke's lengthy discussion of the mission to the Gentiles through following Paul's ministry. This chapter will remedy to some extent the neglect of Paul in this study. Paul proves to be the paradigmatic missionary for the church today. Yet it will probably surprise the reader to discover the lengthy process necessary in Paul's moving from particularism to universalism. The final chapter will look at a pastoral issue that touches on the fundamental nature of the church in the first century, table-fellowship. What role did table-fellowship play in the mission to the Gentiles and how does this relate to the mission of the church today?

7

The Apostles:
Models For Frontier Missions?

Questions to Consider before
Reading this Chapter

*Your mission society has assigned you to work as a missionary among the Weiger people in Northwest China. After two years among this people you have learned their language. What insights can you draw from Peter's growth from particularism to universalism to help you in your mission?

*Respond to this comment: "Peter's example in the book of Acts reveals the reluctance of the apostles in preaching the good news to Gentiles."

An interpretation of the early history of Christianity that sees the apostles as disobedient or at least as reluctant to obey the Great Commission is enjoying popularity among some missiologists. Richardson argues that the "hidden" message of Acts is Luke's intention to show that God bypassed the apostles because they would not go to the Gentiles. He says: "Hundreds of millions of Christians think that Luke's Acts of the Apostles records the 12 apostles' obedience to the Great Commission. Actually it records their reluctance to obey it" (1992:A-110). The argument goes something like this: One reason Luke wrote the book of Acts was to show the unwillingness of the apostles to carry out a mission to the Gentiles in spite of Jesus' explicit commission to evangelize the world. This interpretation is confirmed by the following facts: The first evangelization of Gentiles by any of the apostles occurs almost ten years after the giving of the commission (Ac 10). And even here Peter shows himself reluctant to preach to Cornelius. Also, after the conversion of Cornelius and his household the apostles show no understanding of their call to evangelize Gentiles. Finally, Luke drops the apostles from his narrative and focuses exclusively on Paul who takes the gospel to the Gentiles.

This interpretation of Luke's story of early Christianity, so the argument goes, is confirmed in the letter Paul wrote to the Galatians. Paul reports that he was called to the Gentiles and the apostles were called to the Jews: " . . . they say that I had been entrusted with the task of preaching the gospel to the Gentiles, just as Peter had been to the Jews. For God, who was at work in the ministry of Peter as an apostle to the Jews, was also at work in my ministry as an apostle to the Gentiles" (Ga 2:7-8).

What can be said about this interpretation of the role of the apostles in early Christianity? If correct, it would leave the apostles as negative models for frontier missions. This chapter will challenge this interpretation of the "hidden" message of Acts by showing that Luke presents the apostles as positive and realistic models for those committed to frontier missions. We will begin by examining briefly the flow of Luke's entire narrative of early Christianity with a focus on the apostolic Twelve. Luke's narrative reveals the vital role the apostles play in the mission to the Gentiles. This chapter will also demonstrate that the mission to the Gentiles occurred through a process. Those committed to frontier missions today will discover the realistic challenge involved in this call through an understanding of this process.

The Gospel of Luke

The intense study of Luke's writings in the past century has led to the consensus that Luke wrote one book, not two. This book can be called Luke-Acts. Those who interpret one of Luke's volumes must keep in mind the unity and coherence of his narrative. The Gospel of Luke can be adequately understood only when it is recognized that Luke's story does not end with the giving of the Great Commission as do the other Gospels, but rather with Paul in prison in Rome. Also, any part of volume two (Acts) must be interpreted in light of a story that begins with the visit of the angel to Zachariah in Luke 1.

The Particularism of Luke's Gospel

Recent studies of Luke's writings have confirmed that Luke-Acts is much more Jewish than previously recognized. For Luke the entire story of Christianity is rooted in Jewishness. In his first volume he demonstrates that Jesus' entire life, including his birth, ministry and death, took place in a Jewish context. The particularism of Jesus' life and ministry is striking in Luke's gospel. Luke omits many of the more obviously mission stories found within the other Gospels. Luke follows Mark's gospel rather closely until Mark 7 where Jesus "makes all foods clean" and where he encounters and ministers to a Gentile woman of the Syro-Phoenician culture. Further, Luke omits any mention of the gospel being preached in the whole world until the very end of his gospel (cp. Mk 13:10; 14:9).

How Jesus Challenges Jewish Particularism

This is not to say that Luke does not lay a foundation for the mission to the Gentiles in his first volume. But he does it much more subtly. Jesus remains within Palestine in the Gospel of Luke. Here Jesus ministers to women, tax collectors, sinners, Samaritans and even to a Gentile. But in every instance these are people who are inside Palestine with the Samaritans and the Gentile being very devout and even examples of spirituality (Lk 9:51ff.; 10:25-37; 17:11-19; 7:1-10). The first passage cited shows the Samaritans refusing Jesus passage through a Samaritan village. In this instance Luke recounts the story not to rebuke the Samaritans but to show the need of the disciples of Jesus. They want to roast these Samaritans in Elijah-like fashion. Jesus rebukes their narrow particularistic worldview.

Jesus lays a foundation for a mission to the Gentiles by staying within Palestine and challenging the particularism of the Jewish faith of the first century. The Jewish concern for holiness and purity led them to build such high walls between themselves and sinners that they were unable to fulfill their calling to bless all the nations of the earth. The model for Jesus' ministry in the Gospel of Luke can be found in the Scriptures. Jesus did not go beyond what was modeled in the Old Testament by such prophets as Elijah and Elisha. These men were called as prophets to Israel but ministered to non-Jews only when they came into contact with them. Jesus did the same. Jesus remains ritually pure while challenging first-century Jewish particularism. His explicit call for mission to the Gentiles only occurs in his very final moments with his apostles.

Jesus Lays a Foundation for Blessing the Nations

What has Luke accomplished at the conclusion of his first volume? Jesus comes into the world in the stream of salvation history. His birth fulfills Scripture and he is raised as an orthodox Jew. His ministry, while particularistic, calls into question first-century Jewish interpretations of particularism. He does this by ministering to women, tax collectors, Samaritans and many others who lived on the margins of first-century Jewish faith. These marginals are attracted to Jesus and feel comfortable around him. He, in turn, responds to their needs by forgiving their sins, healing their diseases and confronting their demons. His response to mainstream Jewish faith is one of constant confrontation, challenge and rebuke. Thus, in volume one Luke has laid a solid foundation on which a mission to the Gentiles can occur. A process has been set in motion. This process flows out of the story of salvation history moving from particularism to universalism.

The Acts of the Apostles

The ministry of the apostles after Jesus' ascension is recounted by Luke in Acts 1–6:7; 8:14-25; 9:26; 9:32–11:18; 12:1-24; 15:5-36. During this time the only ministry to the Gentiles occurs through Peter's ministry to Cornelius (9:32–11:18). Does this not confirm the accusation of those who see the apostles as reluctant to obey the great commission? A closer look at the apostolic Twelve will reveal Luke's high regard of their place in the mission to the Gentiles.

Acts 1–6: The Twelve are Jesus' Successors

Luke shows the apostles extending the mission begun by Jesus. Luke begins volume two by connecting the two volumes and then recounting a second version of the Great Commission. This second version is given in the context of the apostles' question as to whether Jesus was going to establish the kingdom. Jesus tells his disciples that there will be an indeterminate time period between his ascension and the parousia. This period draws its meaning from the witness that must be carried out to the "ends of the earth."

After Jesus' ascension Luke gives an account of the apostolic replacement (1:12-26). While all studies of Acts 1 give a great deal of attention to the first eleven verses of Acts, some give little attention to the final fifteen verses. An understanding of Luke's interest in apostleship is important in seeing the role of the apostles in the mission to the Gentiles. Acts 1:12-26 contains Luke's core definition of apostleship. Only those disciples who have accompanied Jesus from the baptism of John are qualified to replace Judas. This explains why Luke almost uniformly reserves the title apostle for the Twelve (Dollar 1993b:188-220).

The core meaning of apostleship for Luke is found in the twelve Jesus selected to be with him throughout his incarnation. The apostolic Twelve must be complete because this group authenticates the new movement begun by Jesus Christ. The apostles extend Jesus' mission. Jesus' mission of teaching and doing the works of God laid the foundation for a new paradigm for mission. The apostolic twelve extend this mission and clarify and confirm this new paradigm (Ac 1:1-5).

Chapters 2 through 5 demonstrate that these twelve men are the true successors of Jesus. While all of the early disciples are involved in witnessing to Jesus, Luke makes it clear that the power of Jesus resides in these men in a special way. Peter leads 3000 men and women to embrace the Messiah on the day of Pentecost. This event is not atypical of what occurs throughout these early chapters as Luke shows the apostles preaching to large crowds of Jews and to the Sanhedrin.

Another way Luke shows the centrality of the apostles is in their teaching. As Jesus was the primary teacher in the Gospel of Luke, so the apostles are the primary teachers in the beginnings of Acts. These new disciples "devoted themselves to the *apostles'* teaching" (emphasis mine). The Jewish authorities are continually upset with the apostles because they are teaching in the temple about the resurrection (4:2, 7, 18; 5:28).

Luke also attributes all of the "signs and wonders" to the apostles in these opening chapters of Acts. "Everyone was filled with awe, and many wonders and miraculous signs were done by the apostles" (2:43). Acts 3 shows Peter and John healing the cripple at the "beautiful gate." Acts 5:12 says: "The apostles performed many miraculous signs and wonders among the people." This is followed by an account of people being healed by merely allowing Peter's shadow to fall on them (5:15-16).

The final way that Luke shows the centrality of the apostles is the degree to which all the finances of the movement were controlled by the apostles. This is so obvious that an idiom developed which bears this out. The ritual for giving in the early church is described as people bringing their gifts and "laying them at the apostles' feet" (4:35, 37; 5:2). Thus, Luke makes it clear that all of the leadership power in the early church resided in the hands of the apostles. The first major power-sharing occurs when the apostles turn the finances of the church over to the Seven (Ac 6:1-7).

The Role of the Apostles During the Transition Period

Luke pulls the apostles off center stage of salvation history after he introduces the Seven in chapter 6. From this time on the apostles will share the spotlight with others and finally will disappear completely from Luke's narrative after Acts 15. What role do they play in Luke's narrative during this transitional period?

Peter and John Minister to Samaritans

The next time the apostles appear in Acts is during Philip's ministry in Samaria. Philip has been used to start a large people movement to Christ in Samaria (8:4-13). In this context Luke brings the apostles back into the story. The apostles in Jerusalem send Peter and John to Samaria where they enable the Samaritans in receiving the Holy Spirit. Luke's point is that the gospel extends to Samaritans through the mediation of the apostles. Although Philip was the first to minister to the Samaritans, his ministry is legitimated by the apostles. When the apostles return to Jerusalem, they preach the gospel in each Samaritan village through which they pass (8:25).

Peter's Paradigmatic Ministry—Blessing the Nations

The next appearance of the apostles again focuses on Peter's ministry in authenticating the mission to the Gentiles (9:32–11:18). Luke recounts Peter's ministry to Cornelius and his household followed by a debriefing in Jerusalem where the entire Jewish church concludes that "God has granted even the Gentiles repentance unto life" (11:18). Why do I call this the paradigmatic event in the mission to the Gentiles? There are a number of reasons that this is a decisive event in Luke's narrative of early Christianity. But before proceeding with these reasons we need to look at the issue of chronology as it bears on the mission to the Gentiles.

The Time of Cornelius' Conversion

Luke places Cornelius' conversion after the conversion of Saul and before the origin of the Gentile church in Antioch. Normally Luke's narrative follows a chronological order. Philip's ministry (8:4-40), Saul's conversion (9:1-31) and the mission in Antioch (11:19-30) are tied directly to the death of Stephen (8:4; 9:1; 11:19). Peter's ministry, on the other hand, occurs in an indeterminate period of time. Luke simply says, "*As* Peter traveled about the country, he went to visit the saints in Lydda" (italics mine). Does this vague reference give any clue as to the time of Peter's ministry to Gentiles?

The impression gained from Acts 9:32-43 is that Peter feels no urgency to return to Jerusalem. This is quite different from what was seen in the first eight chapters of Acts. During this period of time the apostles, and especially Peter, are absolutely indispensable in the church in Jerusalem. Further, Luke notes that in the intensified persecution arising out of Stephen's martyrdom all of the Christians are scattered out of Jerusalem "except the apostles" (8:1). When Philip has a breakthrough in Samaria the news comes to the *apostles* in Jerusalem. After a very brief ministry in Samaria, Peter and John return to Jerusalem (8:25). Finally, when Saul returns to Jerusalem, three years after his conversion, he meets the apostles (9:27).

Moving forward to 11:30 when Barnabas and Saul take a offering from the Antiochean church to the Jerusalem church they give the money to the *elders*. This passage along with Peter's statement after his escape from prison to give a message to *James* indicates that there has been a leadership change in Jerusalem during this time (12:17). The apostles (at least Peter) are no longer functioning as resident leaders in the church in Jerusalem. While Jerusalem may remain their headquarters, the apostles no longer have the responsibility of daily leadership. The apostles were leading the church after Saul's return to Jerusalem (9:26ff.), but were not leading the church when Barnabas and Saul took the gift to Jerusalem (11:27ff.).

Returning to the indeterminate *as* in 9:32, it now seems apparent that Peter is engaged in some kind of itinerant ministry outside of Jerusalem and is no longer involved in the leadership of any local church. Barnabas and Saul visited Jerusalem around A.D. 46 and were launched on their first mission trip soon after their return from Jerusalem. Saul's visit to Jerusalem after his conversion probably occurred around A.D. 36. Thus Peter's mission to the Gentiles, i.e., Cornelius, can be dated with some degree of confidence to approximately A.D. 40. If this is correct, then the first datable instance of direct ministry to Gentiles by the church occurred some ten years after Jesus gave the Great Commission to his apostles.

Breaking out of Particularism and Blessing the Nations

The manner in which Peter's mission to the Gentiles occurred seems to confirm the view of those who see the apostles as reluctant in fulfilling the Great Commission. Let us review briefly how this mission unfolded, looking at it from Peter's experience. Peter is staying in the home of a tanner in Joppa when he has a vision of a sheet let down out of heaven (10:9-23). He looks in the sheet and sees various kinds of unclean (to a Jew) animals. A voice tells him to kill these animals and eat them. He refuses but the vision repeats itself three times. As he is reflecting on this vision the Holy Spirit tells him: "Simon, three men are looking for you . . . . Do not hesitate to go with them, for I have sent them" (10:19-20). He invites these Gentiles from Cornelius into the house and the next day they start out for Caesarea (thirty miles away).

When they arrive, Cornelius falls down before Peter. Peter lifts him up and in Cornelius' house Peter finds a large group of people gathered. Peter says to them: "You are well aware that it is against our law for a Jew to associate with a Gentile or visit him. But God has shown me that I should not call any man impure or unclean" (10:28). Peter's final words of his opening statement indicates that he still does not understand what God is doing: "May I ask why you sent for me?" From these statements by Peter we learn the following things: First, Peter's commitment to Christ and leadership of the messianic movement, which has included a ministry to Samaritans, has not disturbed his Jewish orthodoxy. Second, ten years after the giving of the Great Commission, Peter has no intention of leading a mission to the Gentiles *qua* Gentiles. Third, Peter understands that a mission to the Gentiles would violate his commitment to God and would render him unclean in the eyes of God. Finally, this bold apostle who preached to thousands on the day of Pentecost, this man who preached Christ as the only savior to the Sanhedrin, even at the risk of his life, does not know how to respond when a packed room of Gentiles are eagerly hanging on to his every word.

Cornelius then tells Peter of his own personal vision and concludes his story by saying: "Now we are all here in the presence of God to listen to everything the Lord has commanded you to tell us" (10:33). Finally, Peter begins to preach the gospel to these Gentiles. But before he can finish the message the Holy Spirit falls on the entire group and they began to speak in tongues and to praise God. After baptizing these Gentiles Peter stayed with them for a few days.

The Risk of Blessing the Nations

News of Peter's experiences precedes his arrival back in Jerusalem. When he arrives the "circumcised believers criticized him and said, 'You went into the house of uncircumcised men and ate with them'" (11:2-3). There are two questions that need to be addressed here: Who are the circumcised believers, and why are they concerned about the problem of eating rather than the conversion of Gentiles?

These men who criticize Peter are none other than his fellow apostles and the entire church in Jerusalem. Some would like to interpret this phrase as referring to some Pharisaic party in the church in Jerusalem. That this is not the case can be proven in at least two ways. The first proof can be found by comparing this expression with that found in Acts 10:45 where the identical expression is used. Luke refers to those Jews who accompanied Peter to Cornelius' house as "circumcised believers." In the context of the salvation of the Gentiles, Luke deliberately uses the more emotive term for these two different groups. He calls Jews the circumcised and Gentiles the uncircumcised so as to convey the full impact of what occurs.

The second proof that this phrase *circumcised believers* refers to ordinary Jewish Christians, including the apostles, is found in the entire context of the story. Did Peter willingly and of his own initiative take the gospel message to Cornelius and his household? Luke makes it emphatically clear that Peter is an orthodox Jew who does not intend to defile himself by going into a Gentile home. If Peter had been in Jerusalem and the apostle John had been directed to Cornelius, the first person who would have confronted John would have been Peter.

The second question has to to with the issue of eating

with Gentiles. Why was the Jewish church so concerned about Peter eating with Gentiles? It seems the bigger issue should have been the salvation of the Gentiles. While salvation is the bigger issue, the question of ritual purity had to come first, and was vitally related. Historically the Jews were required to eat only certain foods. To deliberately eat foods disallowed by God was a sin of the worst kind, because it was an act of testing God. Thus, for orthodox Jews, Peter's act of deliberately eating with Gentiles called into question Peter's salvation. And with this Peter agreed. Only God's sovereign actions of giving him visions, speaking to him through the Holy Spirit and pouring out the Holy Spirit on the Gentiles while he is still preaching can assure him that the rules for biblical orthodoxy are being changed. When Peter explains all this to the Jewish church, they agree with him that God intends the Gentiles to be saved without going through the Jewish requirements for conversion. Gentiles are saved *qua* Gentiles.

Jerusalem Confirms a Hidden Peoples Ministry

The final contribution of the apostles in the mission to the Gentiles recounted by Luke occurs in Acts 15. This contribution comes in the form of a confirmation of Peter's ministry above. If this meeting took place around A.D. 49, as most suppose, then it comes almost a decade after Peter's mission to Cornelius. Obviously the rapid influx of Gentiles into the church has led to intensive debate over the theological validity of a law-free mission to the Gentiles. The church has met to discuss and make a final decision on whether Gentiles can be saved without circumcision and keeping the law of Moses. After intense debate Peter makes the first major contribution toward a resolution of the question (15:7-11). He reminds the delegates and participants of how "God made a choice among you that the Gentiles might hear from my lips the message of the gospel and believe." He concludes from this incident that the Holy Spirit made the Gentiles clean and that salvation was by grace.

Barnabas and Paul's testimony confirms Peter's conclusion, and with this James agrees by announcing that Gentiles do not have to be circumcised. This decision is formalized by a written statement and sent to the Gentile churches by delegates from Jerusalem. "The apostles and elders, your brothers, To the Gentile believers in Antioch, Syria and Cilicia" (15:23). With this decision Luke dismisses the apostles from his narrative (Ac 16:4).

Conclusion

What can we conclude about Luke's view of the apostles in relationship to the Great Commission? Are they obedient or disobedient? This survey of Luke's narrative demonstrates that the apostles play a crucial role in the mission to the Gentiles. The following are some of the conclusions reached by this study of the apostles.

The Apostles Stand in the Stream of God's Mission to the Unreached

One of Luke's purposes in writing his two-volume narrative of early Christianity is to demonstrate that God willed the salvation of the Gentiles. The Gentiles become a part of God's people without having to become Jewish. Jesus' mission was to lay the foundation for the mission to the Gentiles. Jesus' ministry, according to Luke, took place within the particular. He was an orthodox Jew who carried out his mission in Palestine. He challenged the first-century interpretation of particularism by constantly going to those who lived on the margins of Judaism. He disturbed people of his day by calling for a loving response to those who were not living up to the standards advocated by the Pharisees. He left his disciples with the challenge to remain in Jerusalem where they would be empowered by the Holy Spirit for a worldwide witness.

Jesus' post-resurrection conversation with his disciples, the selection of a replacement for Judas, the coming of the

Holy Spirit and the preaching and healing of the apostles proves that they are the true successors of Jesus. Nowhere does Luke hint that the apostles are disobedient to the Great Commission. Jesus' command for them to begin in Jerusalem does not suggest any time frame. When Luke talks about the large number of people converted (3,000, 5,000 men, multitudes), he shows the apostles healing the sick and casting out demons and tells of their bravery in persecution (even to death), thereby demonstrating that they are doing the works of Jesus. Luke sees the apostles fulfilling the role God called them to do.

The Culture-free Mission to the Unreached can be Traced to the Apostles

A second reason Luke wrote his two-volume narrative was to refute the view that Paul was working contrary to the ministry of the apostles. The ministry to the Gentiles was a matter of debate and questioning throughout the first century and it would be a serious misinterpretation of Luke's narrative to view Paul as the one who opened this ministry. Rather, Luke writes in no uncertain terms that the door to the Gentiles was opened by the apostles, and Peter in particular. Paul is not an aberration in the church, and, in spite of his accusers, is not responsible for turning this messianic movement away from Jewish particularism.

Paul did not begin the mission to the Gentiles; he walks into the stream of this mission. This mission originates in the Old Testament, continues through Jesus and is carried forward by the apostles and the Hellenists. Paul meets the apostles soon after his conversion. He is brought into this stream through Barnabas, who comes out of the church in Jerusalem, and is set apart by the Holy Spirit to accompany Barnabas on the first centrifugal mission to deliberately take the gospel into the Greco-Roman world. Paul's role in continuing this mission to the Gentiles becomes the focus of Luke's narrative, especially after Acts 16:4, but it is portrayed as the legitimate extension of the foundational work begun by the apostles.

Reaching the Unreached is a Process

What we learn from Luke's narrative is that God works as he always has. Just as it took Abraham, Moses and David many years to understand God's plan for them even though he told them explicitly at the beginning, so it takes the apostles a long time to understand God's desire for a law-free mission to the Gentiles. Indeed, it took a good many years of ministry before the apostles finally understood the clear implications of the Great Commission.

In this respect it is interesting to note that when Peter defends his mission to the Gentiles in Jerusalem he never once refers to the Great Commission (11:1-18) Why? Simply put, the Great Commission did not play any explicit role in this mission. We should keep in mind that the great commissions we find in the gospels were written well after the mission to the Gentiles had taken place. In fact, the mission to the Gentiles was the determinant in the apostles remembering what Jesus had said. Standing so close to the resurrection and the crushed hopes of Jesus not establishing the kingdom, it is understandable that the apostles could not "hear" Jesus' commission. When this is coupled with the orthodoxy of Jesus' life and ministry, the absence of any abrogation of the importance of circumcision and the keeping of the law, it is very understandable that the Great Commission was incomprehensible to the disciples when Jesus gave it.

The apostles were slow to become involved in a mission to the Gentiles, not because of disobedience, but because it took time for the new paradigm of universalism to emerge. As this new paradigm unfolds they demonstrate obedience. The mission to the Gentiles would never have occurred without them. They extended the mission begun by Jesus. They opened the door to the Gentiles and affirmed the mission to the Gentiles as the will of God. As to whether the apostles ever became missionaries to the Gentiles Luke never comments, but the traditions of the church regarding the ministries of the apostles would seem to confirm that they were obedient to the Great Commission.

The Apostles are Positive Models for Frontier Missions

The apostles provide a positive model for frontier missions today. Most churches today are trapped in a particularism that blinds them to the urgency of reaching those who have never heard the gospel. This mission of turning the church toward the unreached will involve a lengthy process. There are many possible roles for individuals and churches to play in this mission.

Peter's "conversion" provides a model for missionaries today who are concerned for those who are unreached. Peter went through a major paradigm shift in his ministry to the Gentiles. This involved a long process but was absolutely essential for Jews to evangelize Gentiles (Dollar 1993a). The church missionaries today will go through a long developmental process in effectively reaching hidden peoples.

Personal Response and Reflection

1.   According to Luke, what is the primary role of the apostles in fulfilling the Great Commission?

2.   Explain what is meant by the necessity of a process in a person moving from the particular to the universal.

3.   What preparation would assist the missionary in accepting the people to whom they have been called to evangelize?

8

Paul As a Model
for Frontier Missions

Questions to Consider before
Reading this Chapter

*Consider this comment: "Paul understood immediately that he was called as a missionary to the Gentiles. Unlike the apostles it was not necessary for Paul to go through a long process in understanding the nature of his mission to the Gentiles." Do you agree with this statement?

*Remember your assignment to the Weiger people in chapter seven? How would Paul's model as presented by Luke in Acts aid you in your mission to the Weiger people?

When Paul declared that it was his mission to "preach the gospel where Christ was not known" (Rom 15:20), he challenged the church in every age to keep moving beyond its borders. How did this Pharisee who tried to destroy the young church become the missionary to the world? What was the process that led this young man, deeply steeped in Jewish particularism, to become a model for frontier missions?

Many missiologists and biblical scholars assume that Paul's movement from Jewish particularism to biblical universalism occurred rather abruptly in contrast to the long difficult process of the apostles. This chapter will argue for a different interpretation of Paul's life. Very few studies have focused on the process involved in Paul's movement from particularism to universalism because of his dominant place in Christianity, and because he is usually thought of as the missionary to the Gentiles.

This study will demonstrate that Paul's understanding of the *nature* of the Gentile mission occurred over a long period of time. It was a process involving many years, culminating in what Kuhn refers to as a paradigm shift (1970). A study of this process provides valuable lessons for the church today as it faces the challenge of frontier missions. Almost all of this study will come from Luke's narrative with only a brief comment on Paul's own sparse account in Galatians 1 and 2.

I will use the concept of paradigm in order to show the intellectual, emotional, psychological and theological change Paul had to go through in moving from the particular to the universal. The concept of paradigm as outlined by Kuhn in his study of the history of science has become well known. For a brief review refer back to chapter two.

A mission to the Gentiles that called for an abandonment of Jewish particularism represents a paradigm shift. For 2,000 years particularism had been the paradigm of outreach to Gentiles. The early church had no trouble with a call to worldwide evangelism that included a mission to the Gentiles. They assumed that this would occur through the historic pattern of particularism; that Jesus' death, resurrection, the coming of the Holy Spirit and the parousia would be such Good News that Gentiles would be attracted in large numbers to this messianic message and they would come into the kingdom of God through the traditional pattern of circumcision, kosher eating and the following of the Jewish laws. The only way the apostles and Paul could escape this way of looking at world missions was through a paradigm shift.

This chapter will show that the paradigmatic missionary, Paul, became a missionary to the Gentiles through the same process as the apostles (see chapter 7). Studies of Paul have failed to explore the process involved in his becoming a missionary to the Gentiles. The assumption is often made that Paul understood his call to the Gentiles because of the radical nature of his conversion. This chapter will examine Luke's narrative focusing on the process that transformed Saul the Pharisee into Paul the missionary to the world. The basic thesis is that it took Paul at least a decade (perhaps more) to recognize the nature of this call. Just as it took the apostles a decade to experience a paradigm shift from particularism to universalism, so it takes Paul at least this long to engage in a law-free mission to the Gentiles. This thesis sounds radical only because of our failure to study closely the process necessary in making theological, psychological and intellectual change. New paradigms of this revolutionary nature come into existence through a long process of debate, discussion and pressure.

Saul's Conversion/Call

Saul is introduced by Luke in the context of the martyrdom of Stephen and as an enemy of the Christian movement (7:58-8:3). His conversion/call occurs in connection with his leadership of the movement to stamp out messianic Christianity.

Two issues are in focus when looking at Saul's conversion and call in Acts 9:1-30. The first has to do with the exact nature of Saul's call and the second has to do with his understanding of that call. First, Paul is called to preach to Jews and Gentiles. A hint that something very special is in store for Saul occurs while he is lying in the dusty Damascus road. Jesus says to him: "Now get up and go into the city, and you will be told what *you must do*"(emphasis mine; v. 6b). This is then followed by the explicit command given to Ananias: "This man is my chosen instrument to carry my name before the *Gentiles* and their *kings* and before the people of *Israel*" (emphasis mine; v. 15). This commission has a very explicit Old Testament flavor of God's call of a prophet (Jon 1:2; Amos 7:14-15). The implications of a commission to preach to Gentiles is then clear. But did Saul grasp the implications of this call?

Luke and the early church understood Paul's call to the Gentiles. But *when* did Saul understand that he was to preach to the Gentiles *qua* Gentiles? There are historical precedents of prophets and even on occasion Jesus himself ministering to Gentiles (Jonah; Mk 7:24ff.; also, Mt 23:15). In fact, Gentiles had been becoming a part of God's people from the time that God had called Abraham (Ge 17; Ex 12:38). Even Josephus talks about Jews witnessing to Gentiles and converting them to Judaism (Josephus, *Antiquities* 20:2). But in all of these instances it was either a very transitory event, e.g., the Assyrians in Jonah, or in most instances those who were converted to the religion of Judaism were also socialized into the culture of Israel so that they became Jews, i.e., ceased to be Gentiles.

Did Saul, then, understand immediately that he was to evangelize Gentiles *qua* Gentiles? Lake (1979:192) argues that he did. Referring to Galatians 1, where Paul says that he went into Arabia immediately after his conversion, Kirsopp Lake asks why Paul went into Arabia. The obvious answer: Paul went there to preach. Later when speculating about why Paul had to leave Damascus Lake says that it was because of his preaching to the Arabians (1979:195). With this conclusion Bruce agrees when he says that Paul began "to fulfil his commission to preach to the Gentiles during his visit to 'Arabia'" (1969:243). In another place Bruce says that Paul's statement about going to Arabia was his way of saying that he understood his call to the Gentiles well before he met the apostles in Jerusalem (1977:81). Bruce argues that the Lukan account presents the possibility that Paul immediately understood his call to a Gentile mission (1954:189ff.).

These conclusions reached by Lake and Bruce are based on the silence of Galatians. Paul simply says that he went into Arabia soon after his conversion (Ga 1:17). Bruce's statement that Paul went there to evangelize Gentiles is as speculative as those who say that Paul went there to meditate on what had transpired through his encounter with the blinding light and that he came back with the New Testament in his pocket! Luke, in his account of Saul's conversion, does not mention Arabia at all. Paul, on the other hand, while mentioning it, does not indicate what he did in Arabia. Furthermore, if Saul wanted to evangelize Gentiles all he had to do was to remain in Damascus as this was a Gentile city, not a Jewish one, as the interpretation above seems to assume. The interpretation that has Saul evangelizing Gentiles immediately after his conversion is an argument from silence. Furthermore, the cultural distance between Paul and "pagan" Gentiles would make it unlikely that he started working with Gentiles immediately after his conversion (Ac 14:10ff.; 17:20ff.). Further, if Paul tried to reach Gentiles it would most likely have been in the traditional Jewish way (Mt 23:15).

Leaving arguments from silence, what does Luke's narrative actually say? From the time of his conversion until he returns to Tarsus the only information Luke gives about Saul's witnessing is in the synagogues of Damascus and Jerusalem (9:20, 29). There is no indication that Saul understood his call to the Gentiles as the abrogation of the cultural requirements traditionally made on Gentiles when they became converts to Judaism. How is it that Saul could understand this commission so quickly when it takes the apostles, who had been trained and nurtured by Christ himself, years to understand that Gentiles can become Christians without the requirements of the Law? Whereas Luke's account of Saul's conversion implies the possibilities of a cross-cultural ministry, and no doubt his readers, both early and modern, find this meaning in the story, there is no immediate evidence that Saul understood his commission in this way. Saul's conversion and call are a vital step in his mission to the Gentiles. But subsequent data will confirm that Saul's understanding of the nature of this mission required many years.

Paul's Relationship to Jerusalem

Luke very carefully shows Paul's relationship to Jerusalem throughout his narrative. Saul first meets the apostles through the mediation of Barnabas (9:26ff.). After spending some years in Tarsus, Saul is brought into the movement in Antioch through the Jerusalem insider, Barnabas (11:22 with 11:25). Next Barnabas and Saul take a gift from the church in Antioch to the church in Jerusalem (11:27-30; 12:25). Later Paul and Barnabas' mission to the Gentiles receives the approval of Jerusalem (15:1-35). Finally, Paul yields to the request of James and enters into a Jewish vow while attending the Temple in Jerusalem (21:17ff.).

Luke links Saul with Jerusalem during these years in such a way that Paul's ministry runs in the stream of what the apostles and the Jerusalem church is doing. According to Luke, there are no major differences between Paul and Jerusalem concerning the issue of the Gentiles. Both the apostles and Saul have been called to a worldwide mission. They both understand that this will be realized through the particular. Although the apostles experience this paradigm shift prior to Paul, it is Paul who first grasps its full dimensions. This is confirmed by what takes place at the Jerusalem conference between the first and second mission trips.

Antioch: The Question of Chronology

Luke closes his first account of Saul's conversion with Saul back in his home town of Tarsus (9:30). This is followed by the story of Peter's mission to Cornelius and household which becomes Luke's paradigmatic story of a law-free mission to the Gentiles. This represents Peter's experiential paradigm shift on the "how" of a mission to the Gentiles. Saul appears again in Luke's narrative during the early ministry of Barnabas in Antioch. Barnabas, realizing his need of help, seeks out Saul in Tarsus and brings him to Antioch. This introduces the question of chronology. When did the church in Antioch come into existence; when did Barnabas come to Antioch; and, when did he bring Saul to assist him?

Luke attaches the founding of this church in Antioch to the persecution following Stephen's death rather than to the conversion of Cornelius (11:19). It is Haenchen's conviction that the church in Antioch came into existence before the conversion of Cornelius, but because Luke presents Cornelius' conversion as paradigmatic, then any story of Gentile conversions would possibly follow Cornelius' conversion. This would also account for the very brief record Luke gives on the origin of this first church made up of Jews and Gentiles (Haenchen 1971:369-70).

Haenchen's argument that these Hellenist disciples preached to Gentiles soon after arriving in Antioch are based on two inadequate understandings of the Gentile mission. The first misunderstanding (which will be dealt with last) has to do with culture change. As mentioned previously, biblical scholars and missiologists tend to overestimate the ease and quickness with which the Hellenists and Paul engaged in a law-free mission to the Gentiles. The second misunderstanding, which is directly related to the first one, has to do with the whole complex question of the chronological sequence of events in Acts.

The New Testament writers in general had little interest in chronological questions and the attempts to discover a precise date for the specific historical incidents in Acts continues to be elusive. James Moffat, for instance, in a 1923 article charted the views of some twenty-three scholars on the chronology of events from the crucifixion of Jesus to the death of Peter (A.D. 60-64). Their views on the conversion of

Paul ranged from A.D. 29 to A.D. 37. Bruce in a recent article on "Chronological Questions in the Acts of the Apostles" notes the difficulty of dating events in the New Testament, but says that Luke writes with a greater consciousness of world history than do other biblical writers (1985:273-96). For this reason most of the datable events of world history found in the New Testament are located in Luke's two volumes.

The issue of chronology bears directly on Paul's paradigm shift. The sole interest in the issues of chronology at this juncture of the study has to do with the question of how long it took the church to begin preaching to Gentiles. Perhaps the best place to begin a discussion of the chronological question is with the proconsulship of Gallio in Corinth mentioned by Luke in Acts 18:12-17. This reference falls in the middle of Paul's missionary career and is one of the most easily pinpointed historical events mentioned in Acts. There is some agreement by historians that the date of Gallio's presence in Corinth can be placed very close to A.D. 51 (Marshall 1980:297). Bruce says of Luke's reference to Gallio in Acts 18:12-17: "It is a near certainty, then, that Paul's eighteen months in Corinth lasted from the Fall of A.D. 50 to the Spring or early Summer of 52" (1988:283).

By locating the Jerusalem council at A.D. 49, just before Paul's second journey, and Paul's first journey sometime between A.D. 47-49, Paul's arrival in Antioch is difficult to date any earlier than A.D. 44 and it could have been as late as A.D. 46. Assuming that Barnabas' arrival is placed as early as A.D. 42, this gives at least ten years between the death of Stephen and the origin of the church in Antioch. If this is anywhere near correct, Luke's placing the origin of the church in Antioch with the scattering of the Hellenists at Stephen's death means that some ten years must have passed between their departure from Jerusalem and the report of Gentile conversions coming back to the church in Jerusalem (cp Ac 8:1ff., 9:1ff. 11:19-20, 22, 26; 13:1ff. 15:1ff., with Gal. 1–2). Although Luke's narrative does not seem to leave room for such a large time gap it will be seen that a lengthy time period between the scattering of the Hellenists from Jerusalem and the mission of the Gentiles seems to be the most reasonable conclusion.

This explanation for the chronological sequence of events in the mission to the Gentiles provides a foundation for dealing with the first weakness in Haenchen's position mentioned above. If this understanding of the sequence of events is anywhere near correct, then the unfounded assumption of New Testament scholarship that the Hellenists engaged in Gentile evangelism soon after being banished from Jerusalem will have to be re-evaluated. The chronological question could be resolved by placing a very lengthy time lapse between verses 19 and 20 of chapter 11. Even though Luke makes no mention of such a time period, his narrative seems to allow for some time lapse between the events recorded in these two verses.

Note that in verse 19 these Hellenists are preaching only to Jews, while in verse 20 some of them began to preach to Gentiles. It appears that these two things happened soon after the arrival of the Hellenists in Antioch. If this is so, then why does it take ten years for Jerusalem to hear about this breakthrough and to send Barnabas to investigate? Other news seemed to travel rapidly during this period, e.g., in chapter 8 the church in Jerusalem hears about Philip's ministry in Samaria. Also, it is clear from a study of chapters 10–11 that the church has heard about Peter's ministry in Caesarea before Peter gets back to Jerusalem even though he was there only a few days (cp. 11:1 with 10:48).

But it may be objected that there is nothing inherently improbable about these Gentiles being converted soon after Stephen's death and that Barnabas came down immediately after that, i.e., around A.D. 32-34. But to take this position on the sequence of events would only complicate Luke's record even further. For instance, Barnabas' ministry to Paul in Jerusalem three years after his conversion (A.D. 35) would, then, be impossible (cp. 9:27ff.with Gal. 1:18). This is not to mention the improbability of Barnabas spending some ten years in Antioch before bringing Paul there. The most likely interpretation, then, is the one that places a large time gap between Acts 11:19 and 11:20.

As has been shown already, there seems to be an assumption on the part of many students of early Christianity that while the Jewish church had great difficulty in accepting the commission to evangelize Gentiles, there were some (particularly the Hellenists and Paul) who found it very natural to evangelize Gentiles. There is in all of these assumptions an unwillingness to take seriously the cultural and theological implications of the radical step Luke records in this chapter. It is only barely possible to get Peter to evangelize one Gentile household some ten years after Pentecost, and even then he has not experienced the kind of paradigm shift that will enable him to evangelize Gentiles on a sustained basis. Although the Hellenists certainly have a greater awareness of the culture of the Gentiles than do the apostles, it is highly unlikely that they could pass over 2,000 years of salvation history so nonchalantly and without precedent. The most likely interpretation of the early history of Christianity is that which sees the mission to the Gentiles occurring through a gradual process, whether one is speaking of the disciples of Jesus, the Hellenists, or Paul.

In summary, then, a reasonable reconstruction of the chronology in Acts reveals the following about Saul's process toward a Gentile mission. Saul's conversion and ministry in Damascus and Jerusalem take place from approximately A.D. 33-36. Saul remains in and around Tarsus until A.D. 45, when Barnabas brings him to Antioch to be a part of the movement of founding a church made up of Jews and Gentiles, each retaining their own particularity. This third step brings Saul closer to an understanding of the nature of his call to the Gentiles, but the record does not indicate that a paradigm shift has yet taken place.

The First Centrifugal Mission

According to Luke, the first centrifugal mission, originating from Antioch, occurs under the leadership of Barnabas (13:4ff). Barnabas and Saul witness in the synagogues of Salamis and then travel on to Paphos which is at the western end of Cyprus. At Paphos, the political center of Cyprus, they are summoned to appear before the proconsul because he wanted to "hear the word of God" (13:7). When Barnabas and Saul are confronted by a magician who was one of Sergius Paulus' attendants, Luke tells the reader that "Saul, who is also called Paul, filled with the Holy Spirit . . . " (v. 9). The magician is defeated by Paul, the proconsul believes, and Paul and *his company* set sail for Pamphylia and then to Antioch toward Pisidia where, after witnessing in the synagogue and being rejected by the Jews, they turn to the Gentiles (13:10, 12, 13, 16ff., 46ff.). After witnessing in three more major Roman cities they return to each of the cities, giving structure to these messianic communities, then return to Antioch, Syria, where they report how God had opened the door of faith to the Gentiles.

In two brief chapters Luke has brought Paul to the center of his story, begins to refer to him by his Gentile name, tells of a Roman official who believed in his message, records his first synagogue sermon, and shows him leading a mission to Gentiles when Jews reject the gospel. Paul returns from this mission trip with a new paradigm of mission. He has experienced a decisive paradigm shift. He now understands that the mission to the Gentiles has shifted from the particular to the universal. What are the key events in this mission trip that moved Paul to fully grasp the nature of his call?

The Search for Direction

When the church sets Barnabas and Saul apart for mission, a deliberate, centrifugal process is set in motion. Barnabas, leading this first mission, chooses to go to his home area of Cyprus. That they have no intention of deliberately targeting Gentiles seems evident when Luke says that they are preaching in the synagogues (13:5). Luke records no conversions and no ministry to the Gentiles while Barnabas is leading the mission. When the proconsul, Sergius Paulus, invites them to preach at his court, they have an opportunity to minister directly to a Gentile audience. The opposition of a Jewish sorcerer brings Saul to the front and through this power encounter Saul becomes Paul and the nature of this mission band changes. This mission takes on a more definite strategy.

Paul's Name Change Indicates a Broadening of His Ministry

The name Paul is Saul's "real" name. It is his Roman *cognoman* (Williams 1985:216; Hemer 1985:179-183). There have been many suggestions as to why Luke starts referring to Saul as Paul at this point (13:9). Some have assumed that this indicates a new literary source that Luke is using. Another possibility is that there is some connection between Sergius *Paulus* and Paul. Johannes Munck suggests that it is at this point that Paul assumed this name for himself and Luke is only recording what happened (1966:119). An alternate view, virtually ignored, suggested almost a century ago, argues that this name change suggests that a new thrust in the direction of the Gentiles takes place (Knowling 1967:287; Ramsay 1982:83ff.). Saul the Pharisee who meets the risen Christ on the road to Damascus gains new insight into his call to the Gentiles. At this juncture, while preaching to a Gentile and engaging a sorcerer in a power encounter, Paul takes another major step in understanding his call to the Gentiles. This interpretation would be consistent with the previous argument that Paul, like all of the Jewish believers, does not grasp his call to a Gentile mission until some years after his conversion. After this incident in the Gentile court of Sergius Paulus, Luke will consistently call this man Paul (with the exception of the two instances when Paul is giving his testimony in Jerusalem [22:7, 13; 26:14]). And, of course, these incidents occurred chronologically before Paul's mission trips.

The Jews Reject the Gospel

Luke records three occasions in Acts when Jewish leaders reject Paul's message of messianic faith (13:46; 18:6; 28:28). It is the one that occurs in Pisidian Antioch on this first journey that indicates Paul's full and complete grasp of the new paradigm of mission. It occurs in this way.

"Saul," having just become Paul, leads the mission to Pisidian Antioch where they seek out the local synagogue on the Sabbath (13:17ff.). After the regular service is finished the officials ask Paul and Barnabas to give a word of "exhortation." Luke gives a rather complete outline of this message as it will serve as an example of the kind of sermon Paul would preach in the synagogues (Haenchen 1971:415-18). The initial response to Paul's message is positive. The following Sabbath the synagogue was packed and "when the Jews saw the multitudes, they were filled with jealousy and contradicted what was spoken by Paul and reviled him" (v. 45). Although Luke does not say so, it is possible that this was the kind of response Paul and Barnabas had been receiving in synagogues wherever they preached. But something new occurs in this instance. "Then Paul and Barnabas answered them boldly: 'We had to speak the word of God to you first. Since you reject it and do not consider yourselves worthy of eternal life, we now turn to the Gentiles'" (v. 45).

Paul and Barnabas understand the nature of the Gentile mission. When they say "we turn to the Gentiles," this indicates a radical change of strategy. Prior to this they had been preaching to the Gentiles, but they had not yet "turned to the Gentiles." Turning to the Gentiles in this context means that they will completely abandon the particular and move to the universal. They will preach to the Gentiles *qua* Gentiles. This was like a slap in the face to the Jews.

To confirm the biblical validity of this radical shift in strategy, appeal is made, not to the Great Commission of Jesus, but rather to the Scriptures:

I have made you a light for
    the Gentiles,
that you may bring salvation to
    the ends of the earth.

Paul's paradigm shift is now complete. He understands the nature of his mission to the Gentiles. This new paradigm has been embraced experientially, psychologically and theologically.

Galatians One and Two

Paul talks about his mission to the Gentiles in Galatians. Here he says that this call can be traced to his birth (1:15). His experience of this call came to him at his conversion (1:16). Paul traces his call to the Gentiles to his conversion. But, is Paul arguing for an understanding of the *nature* of this call at this point? He is following the pattern of the apostles. They trace their call to mission to the Great Commission! I contend that Paul follows the same pattern. As they understood this commission only through a process of time, so Paul also took a number of years to understand his commission.

While Paul shows no interest in the process, there are a few good indicators of when Paul understood this call. I will begin by noting when it is certain that Paul understood the nature of his call. In Galatians 2:1-10 he tells of his trip to Jerusalem where he lays before the apostles his law-free mission to the Gentiles. The apostles are in full agreement with this mission. This is the earliest statement by Paul on his understanding of his call to the Gentiles. When did this trip take place? Paul has two specific time indicators in Galatians. In verse 18 he talks about "three years." Then in 2:1 he talks about "14 years later." It is assumed that these indicate time periods after his conversion. Paul, then, clearly understood the nature of his Gentile mission fourteen or seventeen years after his conversion. Thus, the earliest date would be about

A.D. 46 and the latest would be about A.D. 49.

Can any other evidence be found to support the argument often made that Paul had been preaching a law-free gospel to the Gentiles years before this conference in Jerusalem? That Paul had been preaching this message for a period of time before this conference can be proven by his statement that he feared that "I was running or had run in vain" (2:2). But that he was not preaching this message during the years he was in Syria and Cilicia (1:21) seems to be apparent by his statement in verse 1:23 that the Christians in Judea had heard the report that "The man who formerly persecuted us is now preaching the faith he once tried to destroy." He follows this with the statement: "And they praised God because of me" (1:24). If Paul had been preaching a law-free gospel to the Gentiles prior to Peter's mission to the Gentiles, the church in Judea would certainly not have praised God (cp Ac 11:1-3).

Paul's brief remarks about his call to a Gentile mission shows no disagreement with what has been discovered in Luke's narrative. Luke and Paul both make it clear that Paul received his great commission at the time of his conversion. Further, while neither of them are concerned with Paul's process in discovering the exact nature of this call, both make it clear that the call to a Gentile mission represents a paradigm shift of gigantic proportions. Paul's discussion of the nature of this call with the apostles takes place at least fourteen years after his conversion, well after his experience in Damascus, Jerusalem and years in Tarsus, Celicia and Syria. And even at this late date he experiences some apprehension about the response of the Jerusalem leadership.

The People Paul Evangelized

A final word about the the people Paul evangelized will make the process of moving from the particular to the universal even more explicit. Who are the people Paul evangelized? The answer that Paul evangelized Jews and Gentiles is self-evident, but, as will be shown, the generic term Gentile lacks the precision of Luke's narrative. An examination of Paul's missionary career reveals that the answer to this question is somewhat more complex than is usually thought, especially when a close examination is made of the *kinds* of Gentiles who responded to Paul's message. We will note the evidence Luke gives of the kinds of people who were converted through Paul's evangelistic ministry.

Jews

Luke records evangelistic activity by Paul in approximately ten cities in the Eastern Mediterranean Basin (Antioch, Iconium, Lystra, Derbe, Philippi, Thessalonica, Berea, Athens, Corinth and Ephesus). This list includes some of the major cities in this part of the Greco-Roman world that were predominantly Gentile. At the same time there was a sizable presence of Jews present in almost all of these cities. Luke shows Paul beginning his missionary activities in a Jewish context in at least eight of these cities (13:16; 14:1; 16:13; 17:1,10, 17; 18:4; 19:1). In the two cities where Luke does not clearly state that Paul began in a Jewish context, Iconium and Derbe, later information leads almost certainly to the conclusion that even these two were not exceptions (16:1-5). There is also clear evidence that there were some Jewish converts in almost every city. In at least two instances, there is evidence that either a large minority or a majority of the first converts were Jewish (17:4, 12).

Gentiles

The word for Gentiles (εθνος) is found 164 times in the New Testament with 43 of these occurrences in Acts (Bietenhard 1975:793). This word occurs twenty-one times in chapters 13–21. Often it is used in a very general way to indicate peoples who are non-Jews (13:42; 14:2; 15:3). Paul and Barnabas' missionary reports in Antioch, Syria, along the Phoenecian Coast, in the Jerusalem Council and at the end of these missionary journeys stress that God opened the door of faith to the Gentiles (14:27; 15:3, 12; 21:20). An examination of Luke's vocabulary for these non-Jews, however, demonstrates that while he often refers to them simply as Gentiles, his specific information indicates a refining process. They are not just Gentiles, but those he names were particularly religious Gentiles in the orthodox Jewish sense.

God-fearers (φοβουμενος and σεβομενοι)—Luke is the only writer to use this term in the New Testament. Luke uses three different Greek expressions for God-fearers. He uses the expression φοβουμενος τον θεον (10:2, 22; 13:16, 26), σεβομενοι τον θεον (16:14, 18:7) or simply σεβομενοι (13:50; 17:4, 17). There is general agreement that these terms cannot be said to be technical terms within Judaism, such as proselyte (Bruce 1951:215). Although it comes very close to being a technical term in the writings of Luke, the evidence is not conclusive. Luke does seem to reserve this term for Gentiles who had embraced the ethical and moral aspects of Judaism without embracing the theological aspects such as circumcision and eating of appropriate foods (Bruce 1951:215; Haenchen 1971:346; Bruce 1988:202, fn 7). These God-fearers were well taught in the law and in the faith of Israel and were regular attenders of the synagogues.

It should be noted that this term appears in the context of the conversion of Cornelius and at least three times in the first record of Paul's ministry when he assumes leadership of the missionary team. It seems likely, then, that Luke is adding a theological nuance to the record of Paul's Gentile ministry. This theological clarification also has sociological implications. While these people are clearly Gentiles and would be considered unclean by Jews, they would be, however, somewhat more acceptable to Jews than the general "pagan" Gentile population.

Greeks—The word *Hellen* ('Ελληνας) occurs nine times in Acts, and only in those chapters that contain the record of Paul's diaspora ministry. It is used in the singular only twice, and those instances are found when Luke refers to Timothy's Greek father (16:1, 3). In five of the references it is used along with the word Jews, as in "Jews and Greeks"

(14:1; 18:4; 19:10, 17; 10:21, 28). In another passage it is qualified by the term "God-fearing" (σεβομένων Ἑλλήνων—17:4).
Its last occurrence in Acts is found on the lips of the diaspora
Jews in Jerusalem who accuse Paul of bringing "Greeks" into
the Temple (21:28). Does Luke's use of this term only represent literary variation with the normal word "Gentile" or is
he suggesting a distinct category of Gentile?

In three of the references, it is distinctly used of Gentiles
who regularly attend the synagogue, and in another instance
it is used of Gentiles who would be attending a Jewish feast
in Jerusalem (14:1, 17:4; 18:4; and 21:28). Bietenhard says that
"sometimes the word *Hellen* can also mean proselyte (Acts
14:1; 17:4)" (1975:126, V2). Haenchen, on the other hand, sees
these Gentiles in the same category as God-fearers when he
says, commenting on 14:1: "The mission in Iconium, begun
once again within the synagogue, has great success with
both Jews and σεβομενοι" (1971:419). Whether it can be determined exactly how Luke is using this word, it seems evident that he is referring to Gentiles who have already
turned toward Judaism before hearing the gospel and in this
regard they are religiously closer to Jews than the general
Gentile population.

Summary

A probing of Luke's narrative of Paul's mission to the
Gentiles yields insights on the process of moving from the
particular to the universal. Paul's understanding of this mission ultimately involved a paradigm shift. While Paul and
the apostles were keenly aware of God's longing to reach the
Gentiles, their commitment to historic particularism made
their efforts little more than a branch of the Jewish faith.
Gentiles could be reached only through a one-by-one process. Gradually and steadily the possibility of carrying out
the Gentile mission via the paradigm of particularism became problematic. But what new paradigm would replace
this outdated one? Through Paul's radical conversion, his
long years of preaching in Syria and Cilicia, his mentorship

under Barnabas in Antioch, his encounter with a Roman proconsul and his rejection by the Jews, he finds himself embracing the new paradigm of universalism.

This interpretation of Paul's movement from the particular to the universal is confirmed by Luke's vocabulary
for the non-Jewish converts. Even here Gentile conversions
begin with those who are regular attendants of the Jewish
synagogue and only gradually bridges deeper into the Gentile milieu. The mission to the Gentiles does not start with
pagan Gentiles, rather it starts with those who have already
embraced monotheism and the ethical/moral standards outlined in the law. These Gentiles, at least in Luke's record, are
religiously very close to historic Judaism. They have become
monotheists and Luke alerts his reader to this by referring to
them as God-fearers and Greeks. The changes they need to
make to become members of the messianic faith are minimal.

Application

Assuming this interpretation of Luke's narrative of
Paul's movement from Pharisaic Judaism to a universal mission to the Jews and Gentiles, what insights can be drawn
from the story for frontier missions today?

Frontier Missions Represents a
Paradigm Shift in Every Generation

In 1974 Ralph Winter challenged the church to recognize
that most of the world remained unevangelized (Douglas
1975). He argued that the fundamental task of the church
was in the future. Frontier missions alone could accomplish
the task of world missions. I read his challenge to the church
and recognized the truthfulness of his call. During that time
and since I have endeavored to apply this challenge to my
life. But the vast mission enterprise, engaged in many good
ministries, hearing Winter's plea, has found it difficult to re-
direct their mission in order to focus on the unreached peoples. Some have successfully changed the direction of their

mission. New missions have been founded to focus on the unfinished task.

My wife and I have personally experienced the challenge of focusing on frontier missions in our giving. We have noticed that almost imperceptibly, the money we designate to frontier missions gradually becomes money directed to domestic missions. How does this happen? Often missionaries we support shift to domestic mission because of the difficulty of frontier missions or because of a change in their job assignment. Recently we have decided that future monies designated to frontier missions will remain there, *even if* the particular missionary we are giving to leaves frontier missions.

But, to a great degree, frontier missions remains the orphan of the church. Why? Primarily because, practically speaking, many churches and even some schools of missiology view missions as missions as missions. All mission activity is given the same priority in terms of finances, recruiting and curriculum. The process of moving the church from concern for missions in general to a focus on frontier missions requires a paradigm shift. Paul's process of moving from the particular to the universal provides a challenging model for the church today in moving toward this paradigm shift.

Missionaries to the Unreached Will Have to Experience a Paradigm Shift

Missionaries experiencing a paradigm shift from missions in general to frontier missions and who commit to this mission must also experience another paradigm shift in order to effectively reach hidden peoples. As we have seen, Paul experienced a paradigm shift at his conversion and from the time of his conversion he knew that he was called to the Gentiles. But for Paul to arrive at the place where he fully accepted the validity of the Gentile culture and allowed them to become Gentiles *qua* Gentiles involved a long process. Likewise, missionaries today who are challenged to reach the unreached must learn to accept the validity of other cultures rather than being turned off by the very people they are trying to reach.

In teaching an undergraduate class in Acts I have the students read the missionary story of Bruce Olson (1978). A close reading of this story reveals the radical changes Olson had to go through in order to accept the validity of the Motilone culture. One chapter in the book brings this out clearly (1978:147-53). Baffled with how to share the gospel, Olson makes friends with a leading young Motilone who eventually "ties his hammock" to Jesus. Olson cannot wait for this new convert to share his faith with the tribe. But nothing happens. Then the Festival of Arrows arrives and Olson witnesses an astounding event.

Once a year the Motilone gathered together for a special celebration. One of the highlights of this festival is a singing contest. The two contestants lie in their hammocks and one composes a song while the other follows. An older chief challenged Barbarosa, the new convert, to a singing contest. The contest begins by Barbarosa singing the gospel story and the challenger repeating his words. This contest goes on for fourteen hours and Barbarosa tells the entire story of Christianity. All of the Motilone are listening to this contest with rapt attention. At the conclusion of the contest the entire tribe has been evangelized.

But how does Olson respond to this contest? He is offended by the musical forms used in sharing the gospel. The gospel is being preached through Motilone cultural forms. The music, "chanted in a strange minor key, sounded like witch music" (1978:153). This music strikes Olson as demonic. He wants to put a stop to the whole contest. But he restrains himself, realizing that the cultural forms being used are distinctly different from his own culture.

Those engaged in frontier missions will often find themselves resentful of the values, forms and meanings found among the peoples they are trying to reach (Lingenfelter 1992). Today's frontier missionaries have to experience not only a theological paradigm shift similar to Paul, but also a cultural paradigm shift. Paul had to accept porkeaters *qua* porkeaters; some of today's missionaries have to accept "music chanted in a minor key" as a valid form.

Personal Response and Reflection

1. Summarize the process of Paul moving from the particular to the universal in his mission to the Gentiles.

2. What ethnic or social group do you find yourself avoiding? How will Paul's example enable you in accepting and reaching out to this group?

3. Define the term "frontier missions." In what ways should you be more involved in God's concern for this part of his work? Be specific.

9

Table-Fellowship
and Missions

Questions to Consider Before
Reading This Chapter

*Is inviting someone to your home considered an act of intimacy in your family and community? How does the church express intimacy? When have you last eaten with someone whose food and eating habits were quite different from your own?

*What role does eating play in the Jewish mission to the Gentiles? (Read Ac 10:1-11:18; 15:1-35.)

Eating is one of the most intimate acts in social interaction. To eat with someone normally signals some level of social acceptance. Eating is a universal. At the same time eating is one of the most particular acts in a culture. What a person eats, when they eat, with whom they eat, where they eat and how the food is prepared is unique to each culture. In the movie "Mississippi Burning," which deals with the investigation of the killing of three Civil Rights workers in North Mississippi around 1964, there is a cafeteria scene that illustrates the Southern values. Two FBI workers walk into a cafeteria to eat a meal. One of the workers is a native of Mississippi and the other is from the North. The Northerner sits down at a table in the Black section. The place becomes very quiet as every eye in the cafeteria, Black and White, is focused on this scene. The place becomes emotionally charged. The Whites are angry and the Blacks are embarrassed and fearful.

Luke's first volume is replete with information about eating. Jesus, for instance, eats with his apostles, special disciples, tax collectors, sinners, and Pharisees. Jesus also talks about eating as an eschatological act. Eating can be seen as a social act that communicates theological ideas. Jesus arouses a great deal of anger and confusion, as well as admiration, through his activities of eating. A continual question of the Pharisees was "*Why* do you eat with tax collectors and 'sinners'"? (5:32).

In his second volume Luke does not have as much information about eating. Nevertheless the issue of eating remains a basic theme in the gospel going to the Gentiles. Table-fellowship (which included eating) between Jews and Gentiles as Christianity became a universal movement is not a highly visible issue in the New Testament. This is quite surprising. Perhaps the best-known passage is Galatians 2:11ff. But this passage demonstrates how volatile the issue was in the early church.

The vital role table-fellowship plays in Luke's narrative of the mission to the Gentiles requires close attention. The lack of attention given to this issue in the study of Acts can be partially attributed to its seemingly secondary importance when compared to the issue of whether Gentiles have to be circumcised or not (Ac 10:1-11:18 and 15:1-35). The purpose of this chapter is to explore this issue in Luke's narrative with some concluding comments on the pastoral and/or missiological implications of table-fellowship for the church today.

Historically, table-fellowship functioned to distinguish Israel both culturally and religiously (E. P. Sanders 1990:23-28; 272-82). There was a direct relationship between one's eating habits and purity. It was a means of demonstrating Israel's particularism. While circumcision was more important, it was at the same time a private, once-in-a-lifetime, matter. Eating was public and occurred daily. And, interestingly enough for the Jesus Movement, that which had been a test of particularism prior to Pentecost became a test of universalism soon afterward. The decision that Gentiles do not have to be circumcised, while the fundamental issue in salvation, was only one side of the question. It was the second question of table-fellowship that challenged the Jewish Christians to concretize their acceptance of Gentiles. To participate in table-fellowship with them was to acknowledge acceptance in a personal and intimate way. The willingness of Jews to enter into table-fellowship with Gentiles was also a practical test of their theological understanding of salvation.

The Test of Particularism

God's calling of Israel to be his people required them to separate themselves from all that was unholy, unclean and impure. The law was filled with instructions on what was clean and what was unclean (for example, Lv 11–18 and Dt 14). Israelites were told whom they could marry, what they could eat and how they were to worship. Their survival as a nation was bound up with the process of distinguishing between that which was pure and that which was impure. Throughout their entire history they were obligated to draw boundaries that would enable them to maintain a sharp distinction between themselves and other people. In fact, some Jewish leaders considered their survival as a nation dependent on their ability to maintain this distinction (Ezr 9). Their food laws constantly reinforced this particularism but at the same time they had to be held in tension with the universalism accented in God's covenants with them (e.g., Gn 12:1-3).

Rules of Purity

Ini his discussion of the culture of the first-century New Testament world Bruce Malina points out how fundamental the concept of purity was to Israel. The matter of purity was not only important for Israel but an important concept in almost all cultures (Malina 1981:122-52). Most cultures have very specific guidelines which aid them in distinguishing between the profane and the sacred. This process of distinguishing and drawing boundaries usually can be found throughout any particular culture. Most Americans, for instance, would be displeased if an invited guest ignored the silverware and ate his rice, beans and meat with his hands rather than utensils. This would be unacceptable conduct for an adult. In other cultures, such as India, this way of eating food would be considered normal, but to allow the left hand to be so used would be considered unclean. The matter of purity is not an exclusively moral issue but is a concept that encompasses all of life, including time, space and objects. As Malina says: "Human beings the world over are born into systems of lines that mark off, delimit, and define nearly all significant human experiences" (1981:125).

For Israelites purity was fundamental to their way of life. This boundary-drawing task was nowhere more evident in Israel's history than when they tried to determine how they could relate to outsiders in the area of table-fellowship. God gave the Israelites specific categories of food that were appropriate to eat. These had to be worked out in terms of preparation and cooking, with whom one could eat, and when that which was ordinarily pure could become impure.

Pure Foods

Anthropologist Mary Douglas in *Purity and Danger* explains from a cultural and logical standpoint how Israel decided which foods were clean and which were unclean (Douglas 1966). In a subsequent article she continued this discussion on food and in the process answered some of those who criticized her studies of Israelite food laws (Douglas 1971:61-81). Here she addresses the larger question of how food related to other aspects of Israel's culture. She notes in her studies of other cultures: "Sexual and gastronomic consummation are made equivalents of one another by reasons of analogous restrictions applied to each" (1971: 71). From her study of Jewish culture she seeks in vain for this relationship between food and sex. The most obvious relationship, she says, is that between the "table and the altar" (1971:71).

Douglas says there are three rules that governed Israel's eating habits and contends that these have remained constant throughout its entire history: "(1) the rejection of certain animal kinds as unfit for the table (Lv 11), (2) of those admitted as edible, the separation of the meat from blood before cooking (Lv 17:10), (3) the total separation of milk from meat, which involves the minute specialization of utensils (Ex 23:19; 34:25; Dt 14:21)" (1971:71). She stresses the relationship between meats and people and their degree of cleanness in relationship to the altar. She notes that "between the temple and the body we are in a maze of religious thoughts" (1971:77).

Jeremias also notes the relationship between proximity to the Temple and status in Jewish society (1969). From his study of major Jewish sources describing how members of Israel were distinguished, he identifies thirteen separate categories of people within Israel. The addition of Gentiles brings this total to fourteen. Malina, commenting on this study by Jeremias, says these fourteen categories can be divided into seven divisions (1981:132).

Categories of Purity in the Jewish Religion

a   1. Priests
b   2. Levites
c   3. Full-blooded Israelites ("laymen")
   4. Illegal children of priests
d   {5. Proselytes or Gentile converts to Judaism
   6. Proselytes and freedman
   7. Bastards (those born of incestous or adulterous un-
     ions
e   {8. The "Fatherless" (those born of prostitutes)
   9. Foundlings
   10. Eunuchs made so by men
   11. Eunuchs born that way
f   {12. Those of deformed sexual features
   13. Hermaphrodites
x   14. Gentiles, i.e., non-Jews

Borrowing from Douglas's studies noted above Malina concludes: "The categories, like those for persons, derive from *proximity to the Temple* (and the altar) . . . " (italics added) (1981:126). To eat the wrong food could defile a person, thus making it necessary to go through a cleansing process before entering the Temple. Thus eating was a constant source of danger for the devout Jew.

Douglas argues that "whenever a people are aware of encroachment and danger, dietary rules controlling what goes into the body would serve as a vivid analogy of the corpus of their cultural categories at risk" (1971:79). When this is placed in the context of Christian Jews having to relate to Christian Gentiles, a new appreciation is gained of the incredible pressure most of the Jews must have experienced as they struggled with the eating barrier that had been so intimately bound up with their identification as a people. These rules for table-fellowship, in the Jewish religious system, were related to their worship and ultimately their salvation.

How Pure was Israel in the First Century?

As long as Israel remained a free nation and could control her political borders that matter of food, while requiring constant vigilance, was relatively easy to maintain. It was during the diaspora that their commitment to the dietary laws was tested so severely (Dn 1:3-16). In his massive study of the intertestamental period, Hengel documents the ebb and flow of Hellenization that Israel experienced during this period (1974). The attempts of the successors of Alexander the Great to Hellenize Jewish Palestine met with a great deal of success, but when the pressure became oppressive under Antiochus IV Epiphanes, Israel rebelled, not only militarily, but religiously, and formed new "separatist" groups, calling Israel to a new commitment to purity (Reicke 1968:49-62). This intense opposition to Greek culture and afterwards to Roman influence can be seen in the proliferation of parties within Israel during the New Testament period, e.g., the Essenes, and various political revolutionaries, e.g., the Zealots.

Israel's resistance and the persistent intrusion of the Greco-Roman culture kept the pot boiling among Jews. During the reign of Herod the Great, who sought to pass himself off as a Jew, pressure intensified on Israel. The more scholars learn about the life and times of Jesus, the greater becomes the impression that Israel was much more influenced by Greek culture than was previously thought (Hengel 1987). Herod the Great, for instance, was able to change the culture of Palestine in significant ways. This was even apparent in his massive building programs. He built Greek cities throughout Palestine. Even the architectural style of the renovated Temple in Jerusalem was Greek according to Josephus (*Jewish War* 5:184-227). Josephus laments the Hellenization of Palestine during the time of Herod, especially the introduction of the festival games which were held even in Jerusalem every five years (*Antiquities* 15:267-91). He mentions chariot races and various athletic events where the contestants were awarded huge prizes (often performing in the nude), and even animals fighting (sometimes with men). Living in this context began to take its toll on Jewish culture and produced tremendous tension and disequilibrium. This in turn led to the founding of many different movements, all attempting to give answers for the difficulties of living under a foreign power. This illustrates how vigilant a devout Jew would have to be in order to maintain a kosher table. There was constant pressure to yield to the temptation to eat with Gentiles.

The Test of Universalism

Within two decades after the resurrection of Christ, the Jesus movement had embraced the Gentiles who accepted Jesus as Lord into the fellowship of the church. In light of the strategic place that food plays in the process of Gentiles and Jews becoming one people in Christ, what does Luke reveal about the dynamics of their having to eat together? Recent studies of Acts argue that Luke does deal in a substantive way with the issue of table-fellowship. For instance, Philip F. Esler (1987:71) says: "One issue in Luke-Acts towers above all others as significant for the emergence and subsequent sectarian identity of the type of community for whom Luke wrote: namely, table-fellowship between Jews and Gentiles."

Peter's Vision—Acts 10:1–11:18

Esler's study of this passage leads him to this conclusion: "The central issue in the narrative is . . . that Peter has lived and eaten with them [Gentiles]" (1987:93). He says that this whole passage "is frequently misinterpreted and its importance underestimated by Lukan commentaries" (1987:93). "What matters to Luke," Esler concludes, "is the legitimation of complete fellowship between Jew and Gentile in the Christian community" (1987:96). Acts 10–11 reveals the intertwined relationship of table-fellowship and circumcision. As Wilson says: "It is true that these were two distinct problems, but false to treat them as if they were wholly unrelated. Both are closely connected . . . and it is conceivable... that they also arose simultaneously when the Church first faced the problem of Gentile converts" (1973: 176).

Peter's vision in 10:9-16, repeated in 11:1-10, makes it clear that the question of unclean foods applies to both Gentile salvation and table-fellowship between Jew and Gentile. Luke wants to relate the question of cleanness and uncleanness to both table-fellowship and the mission to the Gentiles. In both accounts of this vision the command for Peter to "kill and eat" is repeated along with Peter's emphatic statement that he has never eaten anything common or unclean. Luke's repetitious handling of this vision in his narrative indicates that this vision relates to circumcision and table-fellowship (10:9-16, 19, 28-29, 34-35; 11:4-10). Luke's story of Cornelius's conversion legitimates the Gentile mission by showing that "the social barriers between Jews and Gentiles have been broken down, because God shows no partiality" (Tyson 1987:28).

In her analysis of this passage Gaventa sets out to "demonstrate that the abrogation of food laws and the inclusion of Gentiles within the church are inextricably connected" (1986:112). To receive Gentiles into the community means receiving them into one's home and accepting their hospitality: "To balk at eating with Gentiles is to balk at receiving them into the community" (1986:121). This interpretation of the Cornelius episode is confirmed by the decree Luke introduces when the Jerusalem council discusses whether Gentiles have to be circumcised or not.

The Decree (Ac 15:20, 29; 21:25)

This decree contains four prohibitions repeated three times by Luke but found nowhere listed or referred to in the writings of Paul. This in itself raises a number of questions, assuming of course that it has reference to the question of fellowship between Jew and Gentile. There are only a few ideas and events Luke repeats three times in Acts: Stephen's death, Paul's conversion, Cornelius's conversion, the rejection of the Jews and this decree, thereby indicating Luke's special interest in these persons/events/issues. There are only slight variations in the three appearances of this decree in Acts.

The Four Prohibitions of Acts

15:20   15:29   21:25

1. abstain from food polluted by idols

2. [abstain] from sexual immorality

3. from the meat of strangled animals

4. from blood

All three of these lists contain four prohibitions. The only change in these four prohibitions is that the first listing contains the word polluted which is omitted in 15:29 and 21:25. This term makes this prohibition more general than the latter ones (Bruce 1988:299). All three lists mention idols first and the meat of strangled animals third. The second two listings are exactly alike and the item that appears as item two in 15:20 appears as item four in the two subsequent passages, i.e., sexual immorality comes second in the first list and last in the latter two lists.

There is general agreement that three of the prohibitions have specifically to do with eating and are meant to change in some minor way both what Gentile Christians would eat and how they would eat it (Bruce 1988:296; Haenchen 1971:449). The prohibition against eating meat improperly drained is found in the Noachian commands (Gn 9:4-5), but it is in the law code where the nature of blood is so explicitly spelled out. This makes it doubtful that there is any reference to the Noachian commands in the decree. To eat blood would be like cannibalism, for blood equals life (Lv 17:10ff.).

Sexual Immorality and Table-Fellowship

Although Luke does not clearly state why this decree was given, there is general agreement that it was given to alleviate some of the tension in Jews and Gentiles eating together. Table-fellowship was an acknowledgment of equality and removed the historic boundaries of separation. For Jewish Christians to eat with Gentile Christians would be to acknowledge their full acceptance of them as fellow members of the church. Paul uses this kind of logic when discussing the problem of incest in the Corinthian church. He tells them not to "associate with sexually immoral people" who claim to be brothers (1 Co 5:9ff.). He concludes this instruction by saying: *"With such a man do not even eat"* (1 Co 5:11). So, properly understood, there is a vital relationship between sexual immorality and full social acceptance, whether rooted in Leviticus 17–18 or in the nature of intimate fellowship. Table-fellowship implied such acceptance.

Acts 10–11 and Acts 15 contain the essence of Luke's theological understanding that Gentiles are accepted by faith in Jesus Christ without the traditional requirement of circumcision. For Luke, the issue of Gentile salvation and fellowship between Jew and Gentile are intricably bound up together. Or, to put it differently, circumcision and table-fellowship are soteriological issues.

If this interpretation is accepted, then it is much more probable that the decree in Acts 15 touches on the same theme. In fact, Luke handles it in much the same way as he did in the Cornelius episode. That is, in Acts 10–11, Luke's major theme is the salvation of Gentiles apart from circumcision. The issue of table-fellowshiop, while secondary, is also included as a vital issue. In Acts 15 it is the same. Luke attaches the decree to the decision that Gentiles do not have to be circumcised without telling his reader what exactly it means or how precisely it relates to the main issue of the ab-

rogation of circumcision for Gentiles. Obviously Luke believes his reader will understand how this issue of food relates to the question of Gentile salvation.

Every picture Luke paints of the church in the early
chapters of Acts shows in an unmistakable way the deep, intimate oneness that characterized those early believers. They
were of one heart and soul, they ate their meals from house
to house, and they held everything in common (2:42-47;4:32-
37; 6:1ff.). If this kind of relationship characterized the Jerusalem church, how could it be otherwise in subsequent situations where there would be a mixture of Jews and Gentiles? But for Jews steeped in centuries of the Mosaic law the
step of table-fellowship with Gentiles would naturally involve problems. In fact, the only disagreement registered in
the New Testament between Peter and Paul was over this issue of table-fellowship (Ga 2:11-14) (Sanders 1990:289). Paul
says that Peter's actions had soteriological implications (Ga
2:15ff.). In spite of Paul's horror and disbelief, the response
of Peter (and Barnabas!), while unacceptable, becomes understandable in light of the foregoing discussion.

Missiological Implications

Luke has included in his narrative of the gospel becoming universal an indication of his concerns about one of
the most obvious pastoral implications of this new event: the
vital issue of fellowship between Jews and Gentiles. In the
two episodes where the fundamental issue of Gentile salvation apart from observance of the Mosaic law is developed
by Luke, Acts 10–11 and 15, he also includes the issue of table-
fellowship between Jew and Gentile as a vital issue. For
Luke these two issues are inseparable, given the relationship
that table-fellowship had to purity. For Luke, table-fellowship
between Jews and Gentiles cannot be divorced from the story of the mission to the Gentiles, nor from messianic salvation. It would seem that Luke's thoelogy of table-fellowship
has strong implications for mission as ethnic division and
particularism are almost a universal phenomenon.

The Homogeneous Unit Principle and Table-Fellowship

The homogeneous unit principle coming out of the discipline of missiology has received a great deal of attention during the past few decades and has been one of the most discussed concepts to come out of the church growth movement (McGavran 1988:198). Donald McGavran argues that rapid church growth in Acts occurred because of the people movement that spread among the Diaspora Jews and the synagogue-attending Gentiles. Whether or not one accepts McGavran's thesis that there was a Jewish people movement followed by a Gentile people movement and that Paul deliberately followed up and nurtured these two movements, it is certain that there was a certain homogeneity to be found within the Jewish synagogue. Whatever class of people attended the synagogue, the very nature of this institution would tend to homogenize those who were regularly present (DeRidder 1979:77ff.). This homogeneity was not rooted in ethnicity but in a common language, the acceptance of a common religion which provided agreement on ethics and morality, and on social, economic or employment status. Luke's general description of the Gentiles who became Christians in Acts shows them to be religiously close to Judaism. While the status of God-fearers has not been fully settled from an historical standpoint there is little doubt that for Luke this term comes very close to being a *terminous tecnicus* (Bruce 1988:202, fn. 7). It described Gentiles who were committed to Judaism but who resisted circumcision for cultural reasons. One could become a God-fearer while maintaining all of one's sociological relationships. To become a proselyte was to become sociologically marginalized and to invite the animosity of one's family and friends and even enemies. Conversely, for a Jew to eat with a Gentile was to experience ostracism from his own community. Sometimes we forget the high social cost Jewish Christians paid as the Christian movement became universalized.

Jervell's arguments on the kind of converts Luke describes in Acts would agree with McGavran's conclusions

(1988:11-20). Those who are converted through Paul's ministry and form the nucleus of the church are Jews and God-fearers. For example, when recounting Paul's ministry in Thessalonica, Luke says: "As his *custom* was, Paul went into the synagogue, and . . . reasoned with *them* from the Scriptures, . . . *Some of the Jews* were persuaded and joined Paul and Silas, as did a *large number of God-fearing Greeks* . . . " (emphasis mine; 17:2-4). Luke also indicates that the content of Paul's message here was messianic in nature, linking this promise to Jesus.

Although McGavran views Paul's mission from a socio-cultural standpoint, Luke sees Paul's mission as a theological issue. For Luke Paul was not controlled by a sociological principle but by a theological principle. God willed the salvation of the Gentiles but this had to be preceded by the preaching of the gospel to Jews. As Luke records Paul saying to the Jews in Antioch: " . . . we had to speak the word of God to you *first*" (emphasis mine; 13:46). According to Luke, this pattern, first intimated in Acts 3:26, is followed throughout the history of early Christianity. Even in Rome, where Luke knows that a church has already been established, Paul will not speak to Gentiles until he has preached to the Jews (28:15, 17-28). Luke argues that Paul's missionary strategy was controlled by this theological constraint of the priority of the Jews.

Luke's record of the Christian movement implies two additional thoughts that caution those who use Acts to validate the homogeneous principle. The first is that Christianity, while starting in a homogeneous context, quickly moved into a multi-cultural context and impacted those who had little or no contact with Judaism. Thus the church outside of Palestine quickly became heterogeneous in nature. If this had not happened Christianity would have become little more than a messianic branch of Judaism. Secondly, all of these people, whether strict Jews, who were zealous for the law, or Gentiles, who had little concern for law, were to experience table-fellowship together and live together as one fellowship. Luke presents the oneness of the church throughout his narrative. For instance, while Paul could circumcise Timothy "because of the Jews," he, along with Silas, could also sit at a meal prepared by a Gentile jailor in a Roman context and also walk around in the heart of Judaism with Gentiles (16:3, 24; 21:29). If one chooses to use Acts to support the homogeneous principle for evangelism then one must be prepared to accept the full implications of the Lukan theology of the church. Table-fellowship for Luke demonstrates universalism.

Table-Fellowship as a Symbol of Universalism

Table-fellowship between Jews and Gentiles brings the greatest challenge to the universalism of the early church. The decision of the council that Gentile Christians were required to follow the four prohibitions linked with Luke's account of Peter eating with Gentiles has significant implications for the church. Table-fellowship was a distinguishing characteristic of particularism. Guidelines for eating of food was inseparable from salvation. This is why the Jews confronted Peter when he returned to Jerusalem. The first question that had to be settled for these Christian Jews was not the salvation of the Gentiles, but the "salvation" of Peter (Dollar 1993b:179-85). However one understands the decision to add certain prohibitions for Gentiles to observe, it is certain that these requirements had to do with the relationship of Jews and Gentiles. If Jews and Gentiles were experiencing their salvation homogeneously, i.e., by meeting in separate house groups, then this decree would not take on the importance it does in Luke's narrative. The implication of these prohibitions is that Christians have the responsibility to work out their differences in such a way that the oneness in the body of Christ can be expressed. If table-fellowship is related to soteriology then it is incumbent on the church to move beyond homogeneity and embrace its fundamental universality.

In the early church it was the issue of eating that challenged the Christians to express the true nature of the church. Was it possible for the church to express its true nature by avoiding table-fellowship? Apparently Luke did not think so. Eating for the Jews was more than a merely social or physiological act. When Peter saw that the Holy Spirit fell on these Gentiles he not only baptized them but remained in their house and ate with them (Ac 10:44–11:3). Peter knowingly and deliberately stayed in a Gentile house and ate Gentile food. This action on Peter's part authenticates his conviction that Gentiles were being saved and also gave tangible expression of the oneness of the church. Without Peter's actions the Jewish Christians may not have taken the step of struggling with the free nature of salvation. By eating with them Peter "experiences" their salvation and this experience becomes a psychological reality to him and to all the Jewish church.

Conclusion

While food does not necessarily have the same significance in non-Jewish cultures, the act of eating with someone has importance in all cultures. When I was growing up in the South my Dad would sometimes hire black men to work for him on the farm. They would sometimes take their meals with us at noon. When doing so they would eat their meals outside the house, or at a separate table within the house. This was fascinating to me even though I accepted it without question. Dad would work with a black person, joke with him, shake hands with him and in many other ways indicate their equality. But when they sat down to eat, the black person would never be invited to sit at the same table with the family. He would use the same kind of plate, utensils and eat the very same food the family ate, but always at a separate table. Why did Dad not take the final step and invite the man to eat at the table with us?

Eating, even if it does not have theological connotations in the U.S. Southern culture, symbolizes equality, acceptance and oneness. For a white Southerner to invite a black man to the table to eat with the family authenticates his humanity in some absolute sense. It erases the boundaries that separate blacks from whites. Add these sociological dimensions to the theological significance it had for the Jews and the implications of this act in authenticating the true nature of the church can be seen. For Luke, evangelism may begin in an homogeneous context, but for the church to be expressed those issues that divide and separate disparate groups in most societies must be worked through to the point where the church fully experiences "table-fellowship."

Personal Response and Reflection

1. How does Mary Douglas's discussion of food assist you in understanding the relationship between purity and a mission to the Gentiles by Jews?

2. What is the relationship between table-fellowship and salvation in the mission of the early church.

3. What applications for the issue of table-fellowship can you see for the ministry of your church? For yourself?

Conclusion

What contribution has this study made to missiology, biblical studies and the mission of the church? There are at least eight contributions to the missiological study of Luke-Acts made by this book.

The Contribution of This Book to the Study of Luke-Acts	
Number	Contribution
1	The Progressive Nature of the mission to the Gentiles
2	The "Conversion" of the messengers of the gospel
3	The Jewishness of Luke-Acts
4	The value of an integrative methodology
5	Table-fellowship as a missiological issue
6	Paul's relationship to Jerusalem
7	How to study Luke-Acts missiologically
8	Frontier missions occurs through a Paradigm Shift

1. The Progressive Nature of the Mission to the Gentiles

Luke's narrative reveals that the mission to the Gentiles involved a gradual process over a number of years. Many biblical scholars have contended that the apostolic Twelve only gradually, and some would say reluctantly, accepted the mission to the Gentiles. They have given the impression that the mission to the Gentiles was much easier for the Hellenists and Paul. It has been assumed that Paul's conversion and call alone were sufficient to motivate him to engage in a mission to the Gentiles only weeks after his conversion. This conclusion cannot be drawn from Luke's narrative.

Luke reveals the many steps involved in moving the apostles and Paul to proclaim Christ to the Gentiles. According to Luke, neither Peter nor Paul engaged in a mission to the Gentiles until at least a decade after their call to mission. This understanding of the unfolding of a mission to the Gentiles seems to be consistent with what is known about any process of change. For 2,000 years God had been working within a Jewish context; Gentiles had to become culturally Jewish in order to become a part of God's people. According to Luke the mission to the Gentiles which broke with this pattern occurred only through a gradual process.

2. The "Conversion" of the Messengers of the Gospel

Acts 10 makes it clear that the major obstacle to a mission to the Gentiles was not the reluctance of the Gentiles to embrace the gospel but the theological difficulties Jews had to overcome before they could preach to Gentiles. One of Luke's major points in the two key passages on evangelizing Gentiles (Ac 10–11 and 15) is that the theological barriers to a mission to the Gentiles had been removed by divine intervention. After the messengers had grasped God's intentions, then the universal nature of the gospel was clearly understood and the mission to the Gentiles was launched.

This insight also seems to be consistent with what is known about the subsequent history of the worldwide mission of the church. While the universal nature of the gospel has been accepted in theory, there is the long record of monocultural missionaries continuing to confuse their culture with the gospel. This insight on the need for the missionary to experience a "conversion" before preaching to peoples of another culture is as valid for the missionary movement today as it was for the Jews in the first century. Whether speaking of the apostles, Hellenists, or Paul, the mission to the Gentiles could only occur through a radical change in the messengers.

3. The Jewishness of Luke-Acts

Although this is not a new insight nor is it without a certain amount of controversy, the fact remains that the findings of this study have confirmed the Jewishness of Luke's narrative. Some scholars have wanted to overstate the Jewishness of Luke-Acts. In contrast, other scholars have even accused Luke of anti-Semitism. Despite these extremes the Jewishness of Luke's viewpoint can be seen with clarity in the Lukan portrait of Paul. According to Luke, Paul remained culturally a Jew throughout his life. In fact Paul cannot be said to be the missionary to the Gentiles without qualification. Paul always begins his mission in a Jewish context and with few exceptions the first converts in his preaching mission come from Jews and Gentile God-fearers in the synagogue. Paul works comfortably with Gentiles but he continues to practice his faith with a specifically Jewish flavor.

4. The Value of an Integrative Methodology

An intense study of critical works on Luke-Acts over the past few years has been both uplifting and disappointing. It is truly amazing how much critical study has been invested in Luke-Acts over the past century and a half. These studies have been controlled to a great extent by very narrowly conceived methodologies and, at times, unwarranted presuppositions.

Luke himself lived, worked and wrote in a context of change and tension unequalled in the history of the church. Jews were taking the gospel to Gentiles and the result was a church made up of Jews and Gentiles throughout the Greco-Roman world. Luke's writing is packed with a sense of the Jewish rootage of the church, even though the membership consists of Jews and Gentiles. Luke-Acts is a missionary story. Luke shows that the Holy Spirit keeps prodding the people of God and forcing them to move beyond themselves. This message must be shared and those involved in this movement will always be caught up in moving beyond their ethnocentric and culture-bound categories.

The study of Luke-Acts calls for continued study and exploration. But those who study these volumes should recognize the complexity of the story because of its cross-cultural missionary nature. Biblical scholars and missiologists must broaden their understanding and retool for their study of Luke-Acts. An approach to Luke-Acts that fails to adequately consider its missionary nature and that fails to utilize insights from the disciplines of sociology and anthropology will be flawed. Socio-cultural dimensions must be properly recognized. The missiologist must note the nature of the Lukan writings while drawing missiological insights from Luke-Acts.

5. Table-fellowship as a Missiological Issue

Luke's theology of table-fellowship between Jews and Gentiles provides a challenge for the church today. Luke sees a vital relationship between table-fellowship and the salvation of the Gentiles. The salvation of the Gentiles becomes an experiential reality to Jews when they are willing to sit at the same table with Gentiles. For the Jews table-fellowship was a boundary-marking event. It was a way of maintaining their ritual purity. For the Jewish church, full acceptance of what God was doing among the Gentiles became concrete as the Jews entered into table-fellowship with them. For the Jews, table-fellowship represented both a theological barrier and a psychological barrier. Because of the gospel these barriers could and should be crossed. When they crossed this barrier they confirmed to believing Gentiles the reality of the gospel. Table-fellowship was a test of the unity of the church. As the church carries out mission in a multi-cultural context they must demonstrate the power of the gospel to overcome ethnicity and prejudice.

6. Paul's Relationship to Jerusalem

Contrary to what is normally assumed, Luke's narrative does not view Paul's mission to the Gentiles as an independent mission, that is, an abrupt and anomalous change in the direction begun by the apostles. The Gentile mission as developed by Luke can be traced, not to Paul and the Hellenists, but directly to the apostles. In this connection the paradigmatic event in Luke's narrative is his account of Peter's ministry to Cornelius and his household in the city of Caesarea. Paul's mission also finds its authority in this episode (Ac 15:7-19).

Paul's conversion and call were confirmed, nurtured and mentored by Barnabas. Barnabas, in turn, was a major leader within the inner circle of the church in Jerusalem. Barnabas was sent to Antioch by the Jerusalem Church to consolidate the first major breakthrough among Gentiles. Barnabas recruits Paul to assist him in consolidating and extending this mission. Later Barnabas leads the first centrifugal mission out from Antioch into the diaspora. Even though Paul quickly assumes leadership of this mission, Barnabas continues to be associated in the closest relationship with him. Barnabas and Paul jointly testify in Jerusalem of their success among the Gentiles. Paul's close relationship to Jerusalem continues through the presence of Silas on his subsequent mission along the Aegean Coast. Finally, it is James and the elders who receive Paul when he returns to Jerusalem at the end of his third mission trip.

Luke sees the mission to the Gentiles as an organic unity beginning with the mission of Jesus, continuing through the efforts of the apostles and culminating in the actions of the Hellenists taking the gospel in a direct way to the Gentiles. The missionary journeys carried out by Paul do not represent any break with the mission begun by Jerusalem but rather continues what was begun by the apostles and at strategic points is confirmed by them and other church leaders in Jerusalem.

7. How to Study Luke-Acts Missiologically

The nature of Luke-Acts must be taken seriously when engaging in missiological reflection. The tendency of missiologists naively to use Luke-Acts and more especially Acts as if Luke were a twentieth-century missiologist must be modified. This modification will not represent a loss for missiology but rather a significant gain. Many of the findings of this study, as indicated by the previous six points, demonstrate the ways in which this approach represents a gain.

Luke is a "missiologist" but the nature of his narrative requires a hermeneutic that is consistent with his approach. First of all, Luke's writings are narrative in style. Didactic writings represent more explicit theology while narrative contains implicit theology. Luke's theology has to be deduced from his entire narrative. Luke is writing the story of Christianity from a theological standpoint using the tools and skills of first-century historiography. He is not struggling with cross-cultural issues per se but rather with theological issues flowing out of a movement that has progressed from the particular to the universal. His story obviously contains insights into the cultural issues it raises because his theological categories represent an aspect of sociological reality. Further, the terms he uses indicate his awareness of the sociological dimensions of the story.

This study has attempted to deduce some understanding of the major cross-cultural dimensions in gospel transmission consonant with the nature of Luke's narrative. There has been some uncertainty involved in carrying through this process as few precedents exist for this type of approach. But the conviction has grown that those who understand something about culture, who have Luke's burning zeal to see the gospel preached in all the world, and who have a solid grasp of New Testament studies are uniquely prepared to accurately interpret Luke-Acts. Those interpreters who have this kind of understanding and commitment are bound in time to make sure that Luke takes his place along with such stalwarts as John, Matthew and Paul as among the leading theologians and mission statesmen of the first century.

8. Frontier Missions Occurs Through a Paradigm Shift

The church differs little from Israel in perpetually becoming trapped by a misunderstanding of the nature of her existence. In moving from the particular to the universal the Jewish Christian church demonstrated for all time what God wills for the church in every generation. This movement involved a radical change that can be labeled as a paradigm shift. Every local church is universal by nature; on the other hand, every local church can only be relevant to those around it by manifesting some degree of particularism. In other words, every church must experience continual contextualization. This process leads inevitably to a neglect of the universal.

For the church to carry out the call to evangelize those who remain unreached, it will have to experience a paradigm shift. This paradigm shift will take place when the church realizes that her fundamental task is to bless all the peoples of the earth. Then when individual members of this awakened church carry the Good News to hidden peoples they must also experience a paradigm shift similar to what Peter experienced in preaching the gospel to Cornelius.

BIBLIOGRAPHY

Agnew, Francis
    1986   "The Origin of the NT Apostle-Concept." *Journal of Biblical Literature* 105(1): 75-96.

Allen, Roland
    1962   *Missionary Methods: St. Paul's or Ours?* Grand Rapids: Eerdmans.

Barrett, David B.
    1992   "Annual Statistical Table on Global Mission: 1992." *International Bulletin* 16(1, January): 26-27.

Barrett, David B., ed.
    1982   *World Christian Encyclopedia: A Comparative Survey of Churches and Religions in the Modern World—A.C. 1900–200.* New York: Oxford University Press.

Berger, Peter L.
    1967   *The Sacred Canopy: Elements of a Sociological Theory of Religion.* Garden City, NY: Doubleday & Company, Inc.

Berger, Peter L. and Thomas Luckmann
    1966   *The Social Construction of Reality: A Treatise in the Sociology of Knowledge.* Garden City, NY: Doubleday & Company, Inc.

Bietenhard, E.
1975   "ἔθνος." In *The New International Dictionary of New Testament Theology*, vol. 2. Colin Brown, ed. Pp. 790-95. Grand Rapids: Zondervan.

1975   "Ἕλλην." In *The New International Dictionary of New Testament Theology*, vol. 2. Colin Brown, ed. Pp. 124-27. Grand Rapids: Zondervan.

1975   "ἀλλότριος." In *The New International Dictionary of New Testament Theology*, vol. 1. Colin Brown, ed. Pp. 684-85. Grand Rapids: Zondervan.

Bromiley, Geoffrey W., ed.
1985   *Theological Dictionary of the New Testament*. One volume. Grand Rapids: Eerdmans.

Brown, Colin, gen. ed.
1975   *The New Internatioanl Dictionary of New Testament Theology*, 3 vols. Grand Rapids: Zondervan.

Brown, Raymond E.
1966   *The Gospel According to John I–XII*. In *The Anchor Bible*. Garden City, NY: Doubleday & Company, Inc.,

Bruce, F. F.
1951   *The Acts of the Apostles*. Grand Rapids: Eerdmans.

1954   *A Commentary on the Book of Acts*. In *The New International Commentary on the New Testament*. Grand Rapids: Eerdmans.

1969   *New Testament History*. Garden City, NY: Doubleday & Company, Inc.

1976   "Is the Paul of Acts the Real Paul?" *Bulletin of the John Rylands University Library of Manchester* 58(2): 282-305.

1977   *Paul: Apostle of the Heart Set Free*. Grand Rapids: Eerdmans.

1986   "Chronological Questions in the Acts of the Apostles." *Bulletin of the John Rylands University Library of Manchester* 68(2): 273-295.

1988   *A Commentary on the Book of Acts* (revised). In *The New International Commentary on the New Testament*. Grand Rapids: Eerdmans.

1990   *The Acts of the Apostles: Greek Text with Introduction and Commentary* (revised). Grand Rapids: Eerdmans.

Cadbury, Henry J.
1958   *The Making of Luke-Acts.* London: SPCK.

1979   "The Hellenists." In *The Beginnings of Christianity.* F. G. Foakes Jackson and Kirsopp Lake, eds. Pp. 59-73, vol. 4. Grand Rapids: Baker Book House.

Caird, G. B.
1963   *The Gospel of St. Luke.* In *The Pelican New Testament Commentaries.* New York: Penguin Books.

Coggins, R. J.
1982   "The Samaritans and Acts." *New Testament Studies* 28(3): 423-34.

Conzelman, Hans
1965   *The Theology of St. Luke.* New York: Harper.

1987   *Acts of the Apostles.* In *Hermeneia—A Critical and Historical Commentary on the Bible.* Philadelphia: Fortress Press.

Copeland, E. Luther
1976   "Church Growth in Acts." *Missiology* 4(1): 13-26.

DeRidder, Richard R.
1979   *Discipling the Nations.* Grand Rapids: Baker Book House.

Dibelius, Martin
1956   *Studies in the Acts of the Apostles.* H. Greewen, ed. New York: Scribners.

Dollar, Harold
1981   *A Cross-Cultural Theology of Healing.* Ann Arbor, MI: University Microfilms International.

1993a   "The Conversion of the Messenger." *Missiology* 21(1, January): 13-19.

1993b   *A Biblical-Missiological Exploration of the Cross-Cultural Dimensions in Luke-Acts.* San Francisco: Mellen Press.

1993c   "The Twelve Apostles: Models for Frontier Missions." *International Journal of Frontier Missions* 10(2, April): 59-65.

Douglas, J. D., gen. ed.
    1962   *The New Bible Dictionary.* grand Rapids: Eerdmans.

Douglas, Mary
    1966   *Purity and Danger: An Analysis of Concepts of Pollution and Ta-
            boo.* London: Routledge & Kegan Paul.

    1971   :Deciphering a Meal." In *Myth, Symbols and Culture.* Clifford
            Geertz, ed. Pp. 61-81. New York: Norton Publishing Co.

    1975   "Pollution." In *Implicit Meanings: Essays in Anthropology.* Lon-
            don: Routledge & Kegan Paul.

    1982a   *In the Active Voice.* Pp. 82-124;183-254. Boston: Routledge &
            Kegan Paul.

    1982b   *Natural Symbols.* New York: Pantheon Books.

Ellis, E. E.
    1966   *The Gospel of Luke.* In *New Century Bible Commentary.* Grand
            Rapids: Eerdmans.

Esler, Philip Francis.
    1987   *Community and Gospel in Luke-Acts: The Social and Political Mo-
            tivations of Lukan Theology.* New York: Cambridge University
            Press.

Fitzmyer, Joseph A.
    1981   *The Gospel According to Luke.* In *The Anchor Bible,* vol. 28. Gar-
            den City, NY: Doubleday & Company, Inc.

Foakes-Jackson, F. J. and Kirsopp Lake
    1979   *The Beginnings of Christianity,* vol. 1 (pub. in 1920), vol. 2
            (pub. in 1922), vols. 4 and 5 (pub. in 1932). Grand Rapids:
            Baker Book House.

Foster, Richard J.
    1978   *Celebration of Discipline: The Path to Spiritual Growth.* San
            Francisco: Harper.

Gager, John G.
    1975   *Kingdom and Community: The Social World of Early Christianity.*
            Englewood Cliffs, NJ: Prentice-Hall, Inc.

Gasque, W. Ward
1975   *A History of the Criticism of the Acts of the Apostles.* Grand Rapids: Eerdmans.

Gaventa, Beverly Roberts
1982   "'You Will Be My Witnesses': Aspects of Mission in the Acts of the Apostles." *Missiology* 10(4): 413-426.

1986   *From Darkness to Light: Aspects of Conversion in the New Testament.* Philadelphia: Fortress Press.

1988   "Toward a Theology of Acts: Reading and Rereading." *Interpretation* 42(2): 146-57.

Grant, Michael
1960   *The World of Rome.* New York: New American Library.

Green, Joel B. and Michael C. McKeever
1994   *Luke-Acts and New Testament Historiography.* Grand Rapids: Baker Book House.

Gütbrod, W.
1985   "Israel." In *Theological Dictionary of the New Testament: Abridged in One Volume.* Geoffrey W. Bromiley, ed. Pp. 372-77. Grand Rapids: Eerdmans.

Haenchen, Ernst
1971   *The Acts of the Apostles.* Philadelphia: Westminster Press.

Harrell, David Edwin, Jr.
1975   *All Things are Possible: The Healing and Charismatic Revivals in Modern America.* Bloomington: Indiana University Press.

Hemer, Colin J.
1985   "The Name of Paul." *Tyndale Bulletin* 36: 179-83.

1989   *The Book of Acts in the Setting of Hellenistic History.* Conrad H. Gempf, ed. Tübingen: J. C. B. Mohr (Paul Siebeck).

Hengel, Martin
1973   *Judaism and Hellenism: Studies in Their Encounter in Palestine During the Early Hellenistic Period.* Philadelphia: Fortress Press.

1980   *Acts and the History of Earliest Christianity.* Philadelphia: Fortress Press.

1983   *Between Jesus and Paul: Studies in the Earliest History of Christianity.* Philadelphia: Fortress Press.

Hohensee, Donald
1989   "To Eat or Not to Eat? Christians and Food Laws." *Evangelical Missions Quarterly* 25(1): 74-81.

House, Colin
1983   "Defilement by Association: Some Insights from the Usage of KOINOVS-KOINOVW in Acts 10 and 11." *Andrews University Seminary Studies* 21(2): 143-53.

Jeremias, Joachim
1969   *Jerusalem in the Time of Jesus.* Philadelphia: Fortress Press.

Jervell, Jacob
1972   *Luke and the People of God: A New Look at Luke-Acts.* Minneapolis: Augsburg.

1984   *The Unknown Paul: Essays on Luke-Acts and Early Christian History.* Mineapolis: Augusts.

1988   "The Church of Jews and Godfearers." In *Luke-Acts and the Jewish People.* Joseph B. Tyson, ed. Pp. 11-20. Minneapolis: Augsburg Pub. House.

Johnson, Luke T.
1977   *The Literary Function of Possessions in Luke-Acts.* Published by Scholars Press for the Society of Biblical Literature.

Judge, E. A.
1960   *The Social Pattern of the Christian Groups in the First Century.* London: Tyndale Press.

Juel, Donald
1983   *Luke-Acts: The Promise of History.* Atlanta: John Knox Press.

Kaye, Bruce N.
1979   "Acts' Portrait of Silas." *Novum Testamentum* 31(1): 13-26.

Kee, Howard Clark
1989   *Knowing the Truth: A Sociological Approach to New Testament Interpretation.* Minneapolis: Fortress Press.

Knowling, R. J.
 1967 *The Acts of the Apostles*. In *Expositors Greek Testament*, vol. 2. Grand Rapids: Eerdmans.

Kuhn, Thomas S.
 1970 *The Structure of Scientific Revolutions*. Second edition. Chicago: University of Chicago Press.

Lake, Kirsopp
 1979a "The Apostolic Council of Jerusalem." In *The Beginnings of Christianity*, vol. 5. F. J. Foakes Jackson and Kirsopp Lake, eds. Pp. 195-211. Grand Rapids: Baker Book House.

 1979b "Proselytes and God-Fearers." In *The Beginnings of Christianity*, vol. 5. F. J. Foakes Jackson and Kirsopp Lake, eds. Pp. 74-95. Grand Rapids: Baker Book House.

Lingenfelter, Sherwood
 1992 *Transforming Culture: A Challenge for Christian Mission*. Grand Rapids: Baker Book House.

Longenecker, Richard N.
 1981 *The Acts of the Apostles*. In *The Expositor's Bible Commentary*, vol. 9. Grand Rapids: Zondervan.

McGavran, Donald A.
 1955 *The Bridges of God*. New York: Friendship Press.

 1970 *Understanding Church Growth*. Grand Rapids: Eerdmans.

 1988 *Understanding Church Growth*. Second edition. Grand Rapids: Eerdmans.

Malina, Bruce J.
 1981 *The New Testament World: Insights from Cultural Anthropology*. Atlanta: John Knox Press.

Marshall, I. H.
 1970 *Luke: Historian and Theologian*. Grand Rapids: Zondervan.

 1978 *The Gospel of Luke: A Commentary on the Greek Text*. In *The New International Greek Testament Commentary*. Grand Rapids: Eerdmans.

 1980 *The Acts of the Apostles*. In *Tyndale New Testament Commentaries*. Grand Rapids: Eerdmans.

184   ST. LUKE'S MISSIOLOGY

184   ST. LUKE'S MISSIOLOGY

Mattill, A. J., Jr.
    1959   *Luke as a HIstorian in Criticism Since 1840*. Nashville: Van-
            derbilt University.

Meeks, Wayne A.
    1983   *The First Urban Christians: The Social World of the Apostle Paul*.
            New Haven: Yale University Press.

Meyer, Ben F.
    1986   *The Early Christians: Their World Mission and Self-Discovery*.
            Wilmington, DE: Michael Glazier, Inc.

Mills, Watson E.
    1986   *A Bibliography of Periodical Literature on the Acts of the Apostles,
            1962–84*. Leiden: E. J. Brill.

Moffat, James
    1950   "Pauline Chronology." In *Contemporary Thinking About Paul*.
            Thomas Kepler, ed. Pp. 157-61. New York: Abingdon-
            Cokesbury.

Moule, C. F. C.
    1959   "Once More, Who Were the Hellenists?" *Expository Times* 70:
            100-102.

Neusner, Jacob
    1973   *The Idea of Purity in Ancient Judaism*. with a critique and a
            commentary by Mary Douglas. Leiden: E. J. Brill.

    1984   *Judaism in the Beginning of Christianity*. Philadelphia: Fortress
            Press.

Nickelsburg, George W. E., with Robert A. Kraft
    1986   "Introduction: The Modern Study of Early Judaism." In *Early
            Judaism and Its Modern Interpreters*. Pp. 1-30. Philadelphia:
            Fortress Press.

Olson, Bruce
    1993   *Bruchko*. Epilogue by Janice G. Franson. Carol Strem, IL:
            Creation House.

O'Neill, J. C.
    1970   *The Theology of Acts in Its Historical Setting*. Second edition.
            London: SPCK.

Overman, J. Andrew
　　1988　"Who Were the First Urban Christians? Urbanization in Galilee in the First Century." In *Society of Biblical Literature 1988 Seminar Papers*. David J. Lull, ed. Pp. 160-168.

Porton, Gary G.
　　1986　"Diversity in Postbiblical Judaism." In *Early Judaism and Its Modern Interpreters* by Robert A. Kraft and George W. E. Nickelsburg. Pp. 57-80. Philadelphia: Fortress Press.

Ramsay, William M.
　　1982　*St. Paul the Traveller and the Roman Citizen*. New edition. Grand Rapids: Baker Book House.

Reicke, Bo
　　1968　*The New Testament Era: The World of the Bible from 500 B.C. to A.D. 100*. Philadelphia: Fortress Press.

Rengstorf, K. H.
　　1985　"Αποστολος." In *Theological Dictionary of the New Testament: Abridged in One Volume*. Geoffrey W. Bromiley, ed. Pp. 69-75. Grand Rapids: Eerdmans.

Richard, Earl
　　1984　"The Divine Purpose: The Jews and the Gentile Mission (Acts 15)." In *Luke-Acts: New Perspectives from the SBL Seminary* by C. H. Talbert. New York: Crossroads.

Richardson, Don
　　1974　*Peace Child*. Glendale, CA: Regal Books.

　　1992　"The Hidden Message of Acts." In *Perspectives on the World Christian Movement*, rev. ed. Ralph D. Winter and Steven C. Hawthorne, eds. Pp. A-110-120. Pasadena, CA: William Carey Library.

Sanders, E. P.
　　1983　*Paul, the Law, and the Jewish People*. Philadelphia: Fortress Press.

　　1985　*Jesus and Judaism*. Philadelphia: Fortress Press.

　　1990　*Jewish Law from Jesus to the Mishnah: Five Studies*. Philadelphia: Trinity Press International.

Scherer, James
    1987   "Missiology as a Discipline and What It Includes." *Missiology*
          15(4): 507-528.

Scobie, Charles H. H.
    1973   "The Origins and Development of Samaritan Christianity."
          New Testament Studies 19: 390-414.

Scroggs, Robin
    1980   "The Sociological Interpretation of the New Testament: The
          Present State of Research." *New Testament Studies* 26: 164-179.

Segal, Alan F.
    1988   "The Costs of Proselytism and Conversion." *Society of Biblical*
          Literature. David J. Lull, ed. Pp. 336-69.

Seifrid, M. A.
    1987   "Jesus and the Law in Acts." *Journal for the Study of the New*
          Testament 30: 39-57.

Sherwin-White, A. N.
    1979   *Roman Society and Roman Law in the New Testament.* Grand
          Rapids: Baker Book House.

Sjogren, Bob
    1990   *Destination 2000: Moving the Church into the 21st Century.* Pa-
          sadena, CA: Frontiers.

Smith, Jonathan Z.
    1975   "The Social Description of Early Christianity." *Religious Stud-*
          ies Review 1(1): 19-25.

Stagg, Frank
    1955   *The Book of Acts: The Early Struggle for an Unhindered Gospel.*
          Nashville: Broadman Press.

Stambaugh, John E. and David L. Balch
    1986   *The New Testament in Its Social Environment.* Philadelphia:
          Westminster Press.

Stott, John and Robert T. Coote, eds.
    1979   *Gospel and Culture.* Pasadena, CA: William Carey Library.

    1990   *The Message of Acts: The Spirit, the Church and the World.*
          Downers Grove, IL: InterVarsity Press.

Synan, Vinson
1992   *The Spirit Said 'Grow.'* Monrovia, CA: MARC.

Talbert, Charles H., ed.
1978   *Perspectives on Luke-Acts.* Virginia: Danville.

1984   *Luke-Acts: New Perspectives from the SBL Seminar.* New York: Crossroad.

Tannehill, Robert C.
1986/8 *The Narrative Unity of Luke-Acts: A Literary Interpretation.* Vol. 1: *The Gospel of Luke;* Vol. 2: *The Acts of the Apostles.* Philadelphia: Fortress Press.

1988b   "Rejection by Jews and Turning to Gentiles: The Pattern of Paul's Misison Acts." In *Luke-Acts and the Jewish People.* Joseph B. Tyson, ed. Pp. 83-101. Minneapolis: Augsburg Publishing House.

Theissen, Gerd
1985   *Sociology of Early Palestinian Christianity.* Philadelphia: Fortress Press.

Tidball, Derek
1984   *The Social Context of the New Testament: A Sociological Analysis.* Grand Rapids: Zondervan.

Tippet, Alan
1987   *Introduction to Missiology.* Pasadena, CA: William Carey Library.

Tyson, John R.
1989   *Charles Wesley: A Reader.* New York: Oxford Univ ersity Press.

Tyson, Joseph B., ed.
1988   *Luke-Acts and the Jewish People: Eight Critical Perspectives.* Minneapolis: Augsburg Publishing House.

Verkuyl, J.
1978   *Contemporary Missiology: An Introduction.* Grand Rapids: Eerdmans.

Wenham, Gordon
1981   "The Theology of Unclean Food." *Evangelical Quarterly* 53(1): 6-15.

Whiston, William, ed.
    1987   *The Works of Josephus: Complete and Unabridged*. Peabody, MA: Hendrickson Publishers.

Wilkins, Michael J.
    1992   *Following the Master: Discipleship in the Steps of Jesus*. Grand Rapids: Zondervan.

Williams, David John
    1985   *Acts*. In *Good News Bible Commentary Series*. San Francisco: Harper & Row.

Wilson, Stephen G.
    1973   *The Gentiles and the Gentile Mission in Luke-Acts*. Cambridge: University Press.

Winter, Ralph D.
    1975   "The Highest Priority: Cross-Cultural Evangelism." In *Let the Earth Hear His Voice*. J. D. Douglas, ed. Pp. 213-58. Minneapolis: World Wide Publications.

Winter, Ralph D. and Steven C. Hawthorne, eds.
    1992   *Perspectives on the World Christian Movement*. Second edition. Pasadena, CA: William Carey Library.

Wiseman, D. J.
    1965   "Arts and Crafts." In *The New Bible Dictionary*. J. D. Douglas, ed. Pp. 89-93. Grand Rapids: Eerdmans.

Witherington, Ben, III
    1994   *Paul's Narrative Thought World: The Tapestry of Tragedy and Triumph*. Louisville: Westminster/John Knox Press.

Scripture Index

Acts 13:42–144
Acts 13:43-47–94, 100, 139, 141, 164
Acts 13:48ff.–94
Acts 13:50–145
Acts 14:1–66, 144, 146
Acts 14:2–144
Acts 14:3–97
Acts 14:10-20–94, 133
Acts 14:22ff.–94
Acts 14:27–94, 145
Acts 15–52, 53, 54, 58, 95, 102,105, 124, 161, 162, 170
Acts 15:1–95
Acts 15:1ff.–106, 126
Acts 15:1-21–59,100
Acts 15:1-35–63, 92, 117, 124, 151, 152
Acts 15:2–95
Acts 15:3–144, 145
Acts 15:5ff.–81, 96
Acts 15:7-19–173
Acts 15:8-11–52, 58, 86, 88, 96, 97, 102, 124
Acts 15:12–97, 145
Acts 15:13ff.–97
Acts 15:19–102, 107
Acts 15:20–98, 159, 160
Acts 15:21–99
Acts 15:23–104, 125
Acts 15:24–102
Acts 15:28–102, 104, 108
Acts 15:29–98, 159, 160
Acts 15:30-35–106
Acts 15:36ff.–106
Acts 16:1-5–144, 145
Acts 16:3–52, 165
Acts 16:4–63, 125, 126
Acts 16:14–145
Acts 16:24–165
Acts 16:33–54
Acts 17:1-10–144
Acts 17:2-3–87, 144, 164
Acts 17:4–144, 145, 146
Acts 17:11-19–72, 145
Acts 18:4–144, 146
Acts 18:6–141
Acts 18:7–145
Acts 18:12-17–136
Acts 18:19–52
Acts 19:1–144
Acts 19:10–146
Acts 19:17–146
Acts 21:8–67, 72
Acts 21:17–134
Acts 21:20–145
Acts 21:25–98, 108, 159, 160
Acts 21:27–52
Acts 21:28–66, 146
Acts 21:29–165
Acts 22:7–140
Acts 22:13–140
Acts 26:14–140
Acts 28:15-28–164
Acts 28:28–141

Romans 15:20–129

1 Corinthians 5:9-15–161

2 Corinthians 8-9–64

Galatians 1-2–107, 130, 136
Galatians 1:15-16–142
Galatians 1:17–133
Galatians 1:18–137, 142
Galatians 1;21-24–143
Galatians 2–102
Galatians 2:1–142, 143
Galatians 2:1-10–142
Galatians 2:7-8–114
Galatians 2:11ff.–152, 162

Subject Index

Anomalies–24, 26, 33
Anomalous–25, 26, 35, 173
Anomaly–26, 28, 35
  See also *Paradigm.*
Antioch–53, 80, 93-96, 102, 105,
  120, 125, 134-141, 144, 147,
  164, 173
Apostle–25, 30, 46, 61, 63, 66-68, 71,
  81, 84, 96, 105, 112,113-134,
  152,170-173
  the Twelve–27, 30, 64 , 67, 112,
  114, 117, 118, 170

Barnabas–64, 65, 94, 95, 97, 102,
  105-109, 125, 126, 134, 135,
  137, 139, 141, 144, 147
Barrett, C. K.–11
Baur–10, 11
Berger, P.. and Luckmann–16, 17
Bietenhard, E.–75, 144, 146
Brown, R.–72
Bruce, F. F.–11, 12, 13, 97, 99, 132,
  133, 136, 145, 160, 163

Cadbury, H.J.–10, 11, 14 , 63-68
Caird, G. B.–43
Centrifugal–138, 139
Chronology–134-138
Church Growth–163ff.

Circumcision–18, 25, 34 , 52, 59,
  83, 85-87, 92, 95-108, 123-
  127 131, 145, 152-153,
  158ff., 165
Coggins, R. J.–72
Conzelmann Hans–11, 64
Cornelius–59, 66, 74-76, 80-94,
  97, 105, 108, 114, 117, 120-
  124, 134, 135, 145, 160, 161,
  173
Cross-cultural–2, 6, 7, 54, 57-59,
  75, 80, 90, 91, 133, 172, 174

Daniel 1:3-16–157
Decree/Prohibitions–98-109,
  159ff., 165
DeRidder, R.–163
Diaspora–18, 53
Dibelius, M.–11, 99
Dollar, H.–2, 91, 118, 128, 165
Douglas, J. D.–81, 147
Douglas, Mary–17, 55, 154-156,
  167

Ellis, E. E.–30, 75
Esler, P. F.–14, 16, 158
Ethiopian eunuch–53, 72, 76-78,
  85

OTHER MISSION TEXTBOOKS FROM
WILLIAM CAREY LIBRARY

For a complete catalog write:
William Carey Library
P.O. Box 40129
Pasadena, CA 91114

CHRISTIANITY AND THE RELIGIONS: A Biblical Theology of World Religions, Edward Rommen and Harold Netland, editors, 1995, paperback, 274 pages.
Addresses contemporary questions raised by religious pluralism by looking again in a fresh manner at the biblical data.

CULTURE AND HUMAN VALUES: Christian Intervention in Anthropological Perspective, by Jacob A. Loewen, 1975, paperback, 443 pages.
As an anthropologist, Dr. Loewen is particularly sensitive to the human and personal factors in personal and group behavior, and he is especially competent in describing some of the spiritual dimensions in the development of indigenous leadership.

MEDIA IN CHURCH AND MISSION: Communicating the Gospel, by Viggo Søgaard, 1993, paperback, 304 pages.
A readable and practical synthesis of what has been learned through the new wave of thinking about communications.

MESSAGE AND MISSION: The Communication of the Christian Faith (Revised), by Eugene A. Nida, 1990, paperback, 300 pages.
Sharing the Christian life and truth is far more than using words and forms congenial to us, but strange and perhaps threatening in another culture. This book not only points the way to true communication but is foundational in this field.

ON BEING A MISSIONARY by Thomas Hale, 1995, paperback, 428 pages.
A book written for everyone who has an interest in missions, from the praying and giving supporter back home to the missionary on the field or about to be.

A PEOPLE FOR HIS NAME: A Church-Based Missions Strategy by Paul A. Beals, 1995, paperback, 260 pages.
A masterful overview of the roles of local churches, mission boards, missionaries and theological schools in the biblical fulfillment of the Great Commission.

PERSPECTIVES ON THE WORLD CHRISTIAN MOVEMENT: A Reader, Ralph D. Winter and Steven C. Hawthorne, editors, 1992, paperback, 944 pages.
This text was designed to be the missionary platform of essential knowledge for all serious Christians who have only a secular education. Used as a basis for special courses in over 100 schools.

PREPARING MISSIONARIES FOR INTERCULTURAL COMMUNICATION: A Bicultural Approach, by Lyman Reed, 1985, paperback, 204 pages.
The purpose of this book is to enable cross-cultural missionaries to be more adequately prepared for the task of intelligent communication.

PREPARING TO SERVE: Training for Cross-Cultural Mission, by David Harley, 1995, paperback, 156 pages.
Until the last decade little attention had been given to the preparation of cross-cultural missionaries. This book will make a valuable contribution the growing literature in this area.

SCRIPTURE AND STRATEGY: The Use of the Bible in Post-Modern Church and Mission, by David Hesselgrave, 1994, paperback, 192 pages.
Addresses contemporary issues in missions, mission strategy, theology of mission, mission principles and practices, church planting, church growth and contextualization.

WORLD MISSION: An Analysis of trhe World Christian Movement, 2nd edition, Jonathan Lewis, editor, 1994.
A 3-volume series integrating essential and relevant articles from *Perspectives on the World Christian Movement.*

WORLDWIDE PERSPECTIVES: Understanding God's Purposes in the World from Genesis to Revelation, Meg Crossman, editor, 1996, loose-leaf, 8 1/2 x 11.
Designed as a simplified version of the *Perspectives On the World Christian Movement* course.